UNLIMITED POSSIBILITIES

8 PROVEN PRINCIPLES FOR ACHIEVING TOTAL WEALTH FITNESS

CHARLES KINUTHIA

Wealth Fitness
GROW AND FLOURISH

Unlimited Possibilities: 8 Proven Principles For Achieving Total Wealth Fitness
Copyright © 2018 Charles Kinuthia
First Edition: April 2018

No part of this book may be reproduced or transmitted in any form or by any means without written permission of the publisher, except in brief quotes or reviews.

To order products, or for any other correspondence:

Editing & layout design:

Hunter Entertainment Network
4164 Austin Bluffs Parkway, Suite 214
Colorado Springs, Colorado 80918
www.hunter-ent-net.com

Book cover design: GLOBAL DEZINERS

ISBN (Paperback): 978-1-937741-10-5
ISBN (Hardcover, Dust-Jacket): 978-1-937741-11-2

Printed in the United States of America.

UNLIMITED POSSIBILITIES

8 PROVEN PRINCIPLES FOR ACHIEVING TOTAL WEALTH FITNESS

Acknowledgments

To my beloved wife, the love of my life, Maureen Kinuthia. Thank you for believing in me and seeing more in me than I could see in myself. I have the deepest regard for your dedication and labor to ensure the completion of this project of purpose.

I wish to express my sincere gratitude to my father and mother, Peter and Nelly Kinuthia. They taught me the true meaning of riches: it is not found in possessions, but what is in one's heart.

It is with much love that I thank my brother, Dr. Phinehas Kinuthia, who has instilled in me the importance of courage and self-love. Thank you for always believing in me and pushing me to be the greatest person I can be.

I sincerely want to thank my business partner and best friend, Shane Maguire. Thank you for encouraging me to pursue my dreams and for teaching me that even the encourager needs encouragement.

Thank you to my mentor and life coach, Ambassador Dr. Clyde Rivers. You have been selfless with your resources, time, and love.

To all of my friends, supporters, and everyone who played a part in making the book you're holding a reality.

Foreword

Dr. Charles Kinuthia is a man that I have known to be a true representation of civility and caring about advancing mankind's greatness. He is a Golden Rule Goodwill Peace Ambassador, as well as a World Civility Ambassador. He has traveled to several nations of the world with me and I trust his right standing in all arenas of influence, particularly business and building workable models that enable others to excel.

This book, *Unlimited Possibilities*, is filled with gems that will teach you how to achieve mega success in your life. Dr. Charles does a great job at delivering, what could be, complex information in a very simple and relatable way. Very practical information that the everyday business owner can use today. A great resource for the person trying to figure out the real foundations of wealth creation. I consider Dr. Kinuthia a leading voice in the *"Now"* generation. I highly recommend his training and this book for any institution in the world.

Dr. Clyde Rivers
World Peace Ambassador
Founder and President – iChange Nations™

Table of Contents

Introduction 1

Chapter 1: Take Charge of Your Life 9

Chapter 2: Discover Your "Why" 25

Chapter 3: Develop the Art of Self-Discipline 41

Chapter 4: Visualization: Can You See It? 57

Chapter 5: Set Your Strategy: What's Your Plan? 73

Chapter 6: Develop Your Knowledge & Gifts 89

Chapter 7: Power in Failure: The "F" Word 105

Chapter 8: Takeoff: Time to Fly! 123

About the Author 137

Notes 139

Introduction

Where are you right now in your life, professional or personal? Be honest. It's time for some real self-assessment. Do you possess your unlimited possibilities?

Contrary to what society says, your purpose is not found in your finances or your title. It is great that your entrepreneurial endeavors are successful, but are you experiencing absolute fulfillment at this very moment? Are you living out your destiny? Or do you feel like something is missing in your life? That there is more for you?

Some successful professionals took a leap of faith and walked away from high-paying positions because they wanted more personal satisfaction and fulfillment. No doubt people questioned their sanity in leaving the prestige of their corporate titles and financial perks. However, a fulfilling life is not always about money. While money is important, is it the true measure of unlimited possibilities? Turning your back on your high-powered corporate position can be a risk, but doing so allows you to open doors to endless opportunities you might otherwise miss. Your burning desire for more may be undeniable and relentless, pushing you to take risks, which can result not only in profit, but also peace that comes from living life on your own terms, taking control of your life, and living out your destiny.

The business owner's company has been producing well, keeping the P&L statement in the black. However, it feels like the company has been running her, instead of her running the company. Though the company is doing well, she wants to maximize the business, stay current with the trends of its industry, and increase profits. She wants to take the business from great to exceptional, to expand into more lucrative opportunities. How can she accomplish this?

What about the individual who has no idea what his purpose is but knows it is not found in working for anyone else? He knows he has talents and gifts, but he can't quite figure out what they are. He may be excelling in his nine-to-five job, but he is not truly happy and would rather exceed expectations outside of his present cubicle. He feels as if he is in a box and needs a bit of support and guidance to escape his mundane life. He knows he is destined for more, but what is the destination? That is the million-dollar question.

Maybe one of these scenarios hits home and describes where you are now in your life. Your title and job don't fulfill you. The money in your bank account doesn't fulfill you. Running your business in the black doesn't fulfill you. You've discovered that success, in the form of money or an executive title, does not equal happiness. In fact, some people find that with success, and the ensuing increase of income, they begin to feel like the life they are living is futile, going nowhere. What most people desire is a life of fulfillment and completeness. That is a life of endless possibilities.

Listen to your spirit. Is it telling you that you are fulfilled and content? Or is it saying that something is missing? Can you honestly admit that you are doing your best professionally? People on the outside looking into your life may think your grass is pretty green, but you know there's something more to be had, so you seek greener pastures. The spirit of stagnation may have halted your forward momentum, in life and in your career, and you just can't take standing still anymore. You are a risk-taker, and you feel it's time to pull up stakes.

It doesn't matter where you are professionally or personally, there is *always* room for improvement. The most successful people on this planet never stop growing. They never stop achieving and making history in some way. Good enough is just not good enough, and never settling is the name of the game.

If you are unfulfilled in your business, profession, or personal life, then be glad, because you should not be happy being average. Average gets you nowhere. You were born for more than average, and admitting this is the first step into absolute fulfillment in experiencing your unlimited possibilities.

How would you answer the question, "What is *fulfillment?*" There is no right or wrong answer, as the meaning of fulfillment is subjective, based on whom you ask. If you ask a parent, fulfillment is seeing her children succeed. If you ask a single person what fulfillment is, he may see fulfillment as getting married and starting a family. The person in college may see fulfillment as landing her dream job after earning her degree.

If you are at a crossroads in your profession or career, you may not be able to define fulfillment. So, let me rephrase the question. "What is *not* fulfilling you in your business, career, or personal life right now?" Sometimes, knowing what is *not* working is the best place to start. Pinpointing these areas helps to determine if you are spending time and energy on pursuits that actually hold you back from doing what you were meant to do. The bottom line is that you know something more is out there for you. The need for more means just that… you want more. This is a natural feeling for those who are truly awakened to what makes them tick and have a heightened sense of awareness. With hard work, taking risks, and making sacrifices, success is well-deserved. You are far from greedy or selfish to want to do better not only for yourself, but for those on your professional team who can impact your purpose.

By the end of this book, you will not only define what fulfillment is to you, but you will have already started taking steps toward being fulfilled. It is time to discover who you were truly meant to be. Be excited about this journey knowing that very soon, you will be living up to your highest potential! Everything you were destined to achieve and receive will be coming to you. Don't be surprised if you are a little nervous. That is natural, for you are moving into new territory, and anything new can be a little unnerving. But, think about the wonders of newness. Newness is beautiful. Newness is fresh. Newness has a certain feel, a certain look, and a certain smell. It is expectation. Don't you love receiving something new? Well, look at this new territory you are about to enter the same way. You are stepping into beautiful newness, and that is something to shout about! This book you're holding will inspire, enlighten, and ignite you, as you step into your new territory to be more successful in your business and financial endeavors.

As the saying goes, *nothing in life worth having comes easy*. You may encounter a detour or hurdle along the way. But remember, you don't have to stay on the detour; you will eventually return to the road that leads to your final destination. And hurdles can be jumped over. It's all about your perspective.

There truly is power in positive thinking. This is especially true in business. A positive mind-set can help you attain unprecedented levels of prosperity. A positive attitude doesn't mean that you are unrealistic about challenges. It just means that instead of focusing on the challenges, you look at solutions.

Unlimited Possibilities includes thought-provoking chapters that will help you define what fulfillment is to you and what it means for your life. What is also wonderful about this book is that you don't have to be on your new journey alone. I am on this journey with you, every step of the way.

Once you start living out your goals, you will become more confident and courageous. It is like an awakening in which you begin shedding the fears that held you back, and you see with greater clarity; not only what will fulfill you, but how to make your desire a reality.

There is no limit to the number of people who are destined for greatness. There is no luck involved in stepping into fulfillment. Rather, it means you must stop making excuses about why you're not where you want to be in your life and career, and make it happen! It is time to quit being a spectator to other people becoming prosperous. Get off the bleachers and become a player, creating your own success.

By now, you may be asking:

- Why do I not feel I have accomplished much, even though I went to college, graduated, and did all the right things?
- How did I end up living this mundane life as a business owner?
- What have successful business leaders done that I have not done?
- How does someone go from poverty to prosperity?
- I have a livable income, but why can't I get ahead?

All of these questions and more will be answered in *Unlimited Possibilities*. I will not hold anything back. Instead, I provide you with the knowledge I learned as I spearheaded the successes of some of the most well-known enterprises and brands in the world. I will be transparent, sharing gems of wisdom gained from business experiences and financial ups and downs. In addition to pouring invaluable information onto the pages of this book, you will also receive realistic tools for business success that can be used in any field. I will share from lessons learned, so that you, too, can start on your path to your purpose. You are about to begin an engaging and fun experience, as you turn your passion and purpose into action and move into your destiny.

Let's get started!

CHAPTER 1
TAKE CHARGE OF YOUR LIFE

Control Your Destiny or Someone Else Will

The rich man plans for tomorrow, the poor man for today.

~Chinese Proverb

CHAPTER 1
TAKE CHARGE OF YOUR LIFE

Control Your Destiny or Someone Else Will

It is time for you to take charge of your destiny, for you to be the *driver* of your life! In fact, because I firmly believe in the power of affirmation, I pronounce that you *are* the driver! Repeat to yourself several times, "I am the driver." Keep reciting "I am the driver," until it becomes a part of your thinking and belief.

I have an incredible yet simplistic revelation for you: There is no secret formula for taking charge of your life. That's right, because it starts and ends with *you*. When you decide to be the driver of your own destiny, you come to the realization that you no longer need to fit into a predetermined mold or follow a destiny others have carved out for you. When you understand this, unlimited possibilities begin to materialize.

Self-reliance is defined as "the reliance on oneself or one's own powers, resources, etc."[1] When you are unsure of your destiny, self-reliance seems unattainable. The lack of self-reliance, or self-doubt, can render you dependent upon the validation of others, making their opinions the driver of your destiny, pushing you to the passenger seat or even to the back seat. Giving others permission and power to decide your destiny derails you from taking charge of your life and your true purpose. A. Patricia Sampson, American businesswoman and board member of Xcel Energy, spoke on self-reliance: "Self-reliance is the only road to true freedom, and being one's own person is its ultimate reward." To have the ultimate reward of freedom that Sampson speaks of, *you must first become fully aware that you possess this power*, which in turn, will give you the potential to control your destiny.

Self-reliant thinkers are independent thinkers, being fully confident in their abilities, decisions, and powers, not conforming to society's map for living a successful life. It's quite analogous to everyday life. When you are given directions to someone's home, you have to trust that the roadmap or directions are accurate and will lead you to your destination. Oftentimes, the directions are different from what your car or phone navigation system provides. Which map do you follow so that you don't get lost, but arrive at your destination?

By elevating your thinking a little higher and being self-reliant, you are creating your roadmap of your journey toward your destiny. Forging your own formula for taking charge of your life and controlling your destiny keeps you on the path you created for yourself. You will discover freedom when you no longer trust others to determine your path.

This freedom also extends to your thoughts. The seed of unlimited possibilities is planted when you replace traditional thinking with a more advanced and advantageous mind-set. This should be an "aha" moment for you right here. This pivotal point in time is when you adjust your pattern of thinking, which launches your process of reclaiming and gaining the power necessary for limitless success in all areas of your life.

Are you dissatisfied in your present state? What has brought you to this place? Let me rephrase the question. What has been stopping you from truly *winning*? What caused you to *lose* yourself and your power? Your upbringing, complacency, or challenges all contribute to one's loss of power. Delving deep into the process of reclaiming your power, you must first address the root cause of having lost your power. Only when you get beyond symptoms and deal with the source can you break the chains that have been holding your back. Then, you can begin controlling your own life and destiny.

Remaining powerless can feel normal. You may not even be consciously aware of it. But, it is never normal for independent or self-reliant thinkers to lose their power. They are invariably cognizant of their power and position. Mastering the mind-set of a self-reliant thinker means knowing every single decision you make, not the decisions of others, determines your destiny. *Your* ability ultimately results in boundless possibilities for a successful life, in this moment and in the future.

Do any of these scenarios sound familiar? A potential investor failed to come through, so you postponed the opening of your business. A new team member entrusted with an important assignment failed to meet a deadline and resulted in your loss of a major account. The expectations of your family pushed you into a career that brings you no fulfillment. The commonality of these situations is individuals who have given over the power of their destinies to others.

If you have given your power to someone else, that person who has control of your destiny is not to blame. No! You made the decision to give away your power. Independent thinkers do not put their fate in the hands of another, no matter the pressure they are up against. You never want to be left standing in the wind with no hope, having given others power over your destiny and dreams.

Where you are in life, whether it is in your career or other areas is ultimately because of *your* choices. You wouldn't give someone the only key to your home, so that you have to ask permission every time you want to gain entry, would you? Of course not. The same goes for your destiny. You and you *alone* are to possess the key that unlocks the door to the life you desire. While nothing is wrong with including others as part of your support system, they should never be the source for your promises. Choose now to control your own outcome.

Unlimited possibilities were not something I thought attainable in my life, until I awakened to that reality. For some people, the awakening to the intention of existence has to occur at a low point in life. From my personal experience and speaking with individuals, it is my firm belief that when situations are dire, your destiny can be revealed. It is like a fire is lit within, releasing a spark to greater things. Let's contemplate on this for a moment. When you enjoy comfort and ease—financially, personally, and professionally—are you thinking that there is something more? Most likely, you're thinking how great life is right now. When everything is going well, you are immersed in the moment and not thinking, "What else could there possibly be?" The voice of your true destiny might be drowned out, because of your current prosperity. Your destiny may be trying to speak to you, but your present comfort exerts a more dominant influence. Nothing is wrong with prosperity, and I encourage you to reach your dreams and goals for financial success, but being financially secure does not equal your destiny. Countless people have great wealth, but still suffer with a sense of powerlessness, feeling as if something is missing in their lives. When you become aware of your future and pursue that which you were born to do, you are then in possession of your true power, on which you cannot place a monetary value.

My family did not have means while I was growing up. We were dirt poor, living far below the poverty line. Two words were frequently spoken in my childhood home that still reverberates with me to this day: "No money." This was the answer I always heard from my parents when I asked for either something I wanted or even the bare necessities. We never had money. When I graduated from high school, I did not graduate with impressive scores, which meant no scholarships and no possibility of college.

In my late teens, destiny's voice began to whisper to me. After high school, my destiny became more apparent when I observed my friends living a lifestyle I desired. To clarify, I was not envious, seeing others winning, for aspirations should never stem from a jealous spirit. The seed of my destiny was planted, being watered by the desire within me to have more, achieve more, and experience the best that life had to offer *me*. Looking for a solution, and not being able to turn to my parents for financial support, I attended technical school. But, it was not my passion and only a temporary fix to a permanent problem, so I dropped out. Though I left technical school and had no financial means, I wasn't in a bad place emotionally.

Even though my parents were responsible for my upbringing, being close to twenty-years-old, I had to take serious charge of my life. I became fully dedicated to being the driver of my life. I'd had enough of poverty and, more important, being without power. Though I wasn't aware of my purpose and destiny, I knew it had to be more than my present state.

UNLIMITED POSSIBILITIES

When you are at the bottom, it's true that you have nowhere to go but up. My *up* was selling mobile devices. Though a humble job, it was the start of my taking charge of my life. It definitely wasn't glamorous, but that didn't matter, for it was an important beginning step toward my destiny. Not being where I wanted to be didn't discourage me. Seeing into the future and where I desired to be continued to motivate me. Dealing in cell phones taught me valuable skills that helped me become successful in sales and eventually in the business world. I didn't realize it until I became older, but my early experience in sales taught me that sales would be part of my everyday life.

When you break it down, selling is transference of energy. It's simply helping others solve their problems. Everyone, without realizing it, engages in sales daily. You sell yourself through your job performance to get a promotion. In relationships, people sell themselves to get a second date. You sell yourself to potential clients or customers with the intention of showing them that your product or service meets their needs. To have influence in your field, you have to sell yourself, believing that you are a worthy product to invest in. You don't need gimmicks to have the power to sell yourself. You already possess that power: it is *you*.

I didn't make much money starting off in mobile device retail, but the trade-off was the power I felt. I was finally in control. With specific skills, I became knowledgeable and worked my way up. For every move I made, it was a step up taking me higher and higher.

When you are in command and the dominant force of your life, you decide your course and the outcome. However, when you let things happen by chance in your career or business, you have lost your control to others. You're going along with others' choices, letting them be the driver and denying your destiny.

Realizing this growing power within me, I finally became the driver of my life. This authority didn't come overnight and it didn't come without a price. I had challenges to overcome, and I had to be resilient, determined, and unshakeable in my belief that I would eventually possess the fullness of my destiny. You, too, must be willing to pay the price. Success does not come to the faint of heart. It requires of you the same things it did of me. You will face obstacles that you must address. But, being the driver puts you in control.

Over the years, through my achievements and experiences in business, I created *The C Factor 5Ds* to help individuals become the drivers of their lives, leading them to advance toward unlimited possibilities.

The C Factor 5 Ds That Will Put You in the Driver's Seat

The independent thinker with the spirit of self-reliance knows that she already owns the license to be the driver. No need to ask anyone else for permission to be the leader of your own life, as the only one you need permission from is you. William Ernest Henley once said, "I am the master of my fate: I am the captain of my soul." Already qualified to control your own destiny, start taking charge of your life. Give yourself permission to start walking in this new and exciting territory. To help you, The *C Factor* is a proven formula that will help build you into the driver you were destined to be.

1. Desire to Change

The inner voice that has been speaking to you is *desire*. It has been whispering and encouraging you to release the determination deep within you and to make it a reality. A number of reasons come to mind as to why you have not answered this voice: fear, doubt, and negative influences are all contributing behaviors that conflict with your desire. The longer you allow these attitudes to stifle your eagerness to get on to your destiny, the longer you remain confined and powerless. "Desire is the starting point of all achievement, not a hope, not a wish, but a keen pulsating desire which transcends everything." The late Napoleon Hill, American self-help author, spoke these wise words. If you think about desire as Hill did, you have already won half the battle against any behaviors opposing your desire. The fact that you have a desire means you have started on your road to success and have the potential to surpass any goal you can imagine. I affirm, as should you, that your strong desire has overcome any actions that oppose your success. You possess the desire, but now it is time to release this energy. Once released, you will progress from choosing to change to *actual* change.

2. Determine the Necessary Action

"Failing to plan is planning to fail," is a familiar expression often credited to one of the founding fathers of the United States, Benjamin Franklin. This phrase, often used in business, is relevant to your taking control of your life and graduating from average success to a high achiever. It's time to determine your action steps to take you into a better life. You can't skip this step, for it determines the advancement of your dreams and goals. It is the roadmap to your destination.

You have received your invitation for a prosperous destiny. To obtain it, action is necessary. Some people feel overwhelmed at this stage, but if you break it down into parts, it can be stimulating. Successful individuals flourish in this stage, because they are creating their roadmaps and have total control of how to reach their destinations. The only difference between them and you is attitude. Who better to plan the map for the life you want than the person living it? That person is you!

The roadmap you will create keeps you from being a helpless wanderer through life. This action step is where your imagination comes into play. It requires deep thought and reflection on where you are presently in life and what you must do for *you* to be the creator of your destiny. Don't just work this step; be dedicated to it, understanding that what you plan is a major determinant of your goals becoming reality. It is all about the perfection of your planning and preparation, so be excited about creating your guidelines to win! As you create the action plan for you to thrive in your life, you will experience a shift in your energy. It will be empowering.

3. Deadlines and Action

Your creation of instructions—your roadmap—now transfers from planning to taking action that will bring your epic plan of power into existence. Don't fear, hesitate, or procrastinate with this step. Thomas Jefferson spoke about action, saying, "Do you want to know who you are? Don't ask. Act! Action will delineate and define you." The action you take will reveal the level of passion you possess to control your destiny.

Along with taking action, you cannot forget the importance of deadlines. Influencers and authorities rarely operate without deadlines. Setting time limits on fulfilling goals increases your chance of achieving them. The longer your goal goes without a completion date, the greater the likelihood that it will remain just a goal. Deadlines take you from a goal to a *go*, moving you forward, holding you accountable, helping you prioritize, enhancing creativity, and keeping you motivated. "Deadlines refine the mind. They remove variables like exotic materials and processes that take too long. The closer the deadline, the more likely you'll start thinking way outside the box," said American industrial designer and television personality Adam Savage. For every goal you create, immediately write next to it a *realistic* deadline. Many people are eager to succeed but can fail, not because they were not intelligent or determined enough, but because they either did not establish a deadline or the timeline they created was unrealistic. Don't make your wants unattainable with unrealistic dates that will leave your goals dead. If you have been in business for one month and have turned a profit of $5,000, is it realistic to set a goal to bring in $1 million by the end of the first quarter? While the ambition is appreciable, this is not a realistic goal.

Non-fulfillment of a goal, even if impractical, can trigger fear and insecurity. And when these sentiments surface, it is natural to doubt your ability to succeed. At no time should a goal be set without a deadline, but make sure the date(s) is sensible. As Brian Tracy said, "There are no unrealistic goals—only unrealistic deadlines. The overnight success has usually been toiling in the vineyards without recognition for many years."

4. Discipline/Self-Discipline

Oh, the art of self-discipline! This fourth D is probably the most difficult for individuals coming into this new way of self-reliant thinking. *Oxford Dictionary* defines *self-discipline* as "the ability to control one's feelings and overcome one's weaknesses; the ability to pursue what one thinks is right despite temptations to abandon it."[2] What temptations have lured you away from your life-changing progress? You may be dealing with the distractions of everyday life, individuals who are a negative influence, or thoughts of insecurity. There is any number of temptations, and no two people deal with the same ones. Whatever threatens to hold you back, be aware of it, acknowledge it, and most importantly, turn away from it. Victorious people are always aware of those things that can separate them from attaining their goals.

The impulse to be distracted by other things can overtake us all. However, I said *can*. Just because it can does not mean it will. It all depends upon your determination to go against those distractions. Your willpower and self-discipline must be stronger than those urges that can pull you away from the power to proceed. Never allow those enticements to hinder your journey to success.

The saying, "Old habits are hard to break" is given entirely too much power, being used far too often to make an excuse not to better oneself. Excuses will exclude you from being the driver of your life and the champion you are destined to be. In order for you to be in complete control and the driver of your life, self-discipline has to trump distractions. Any temptation that overtakes your self-discipline is because you have authorized it. That's right! I charge and challenge you today to give permission to the potential and not the regression. Don't allow any opposition to separate you from being in the winner's circle where you belong.

In life, we will suffer two pains: the pain of discipline or the pain of regret. Discipline is the key to obtaining what you want in life. Discipline requires a price, but cannot compare with the pain of disappointment and regret in life.

5. Dream Team

Having a winner's mind-set will make you the master in the artistry of self-discipline. But, don't think you have to travel this journey alone. Ever surrounding themselves with a "dream team" of like-minded individuals, winners place themselves in the company of other winners. And since you are a winner, you must do the same.

You are human, and as you experience life's inevitable ups and downs, your emotions can shift. One day, you may feel like you're on top of the world and the next day you feel like a loser. "The best thing to do when you find yourself in a hurting or vulnerable place is to surround yourself with the strongest, finest, most positive people you know," says three-time Olympic gold medalist Kristin Armstrong. You are in need of those who will cheer you through to the finish line. The winners you have in your circle will work together for all to prevail, whether they are professional colleagues, a business or life coach, or a trusted mentor.

To defeat distractions and be a master at self-discipline, you need a strong support system. All winners need cheerleaders from time to time on their journey, and there is no shame in admitting it, because no one has made it to the top on their own. Your cheerleaders, or winners, in your circle are motivators and accountability partners. They are not to be confused with enablers, who are catastrophic to your calling. You must be strategic and selective in choosing who will be part of your team. Even if they are successful in some way, it doesn't necessarily mean they are a good fit for your team. Not only must they be achievers, they must also be like-minded spiritually, emotionally, and mentally. Your circle should not be *yes-men*, but individuals who are not afraid to be honest with you, giving you constructive criticism whenever necessary. They should help you in your process of expansion and growth. And whenever you are faced with the challenge of old habits or people's opinions invading your independent thinking (which will happen), those in your circle can be a life-saver. Who is in your winner's circle?

My *5 Ds* are a realistic template to help you reclaim your control and the success you are destined for. The *C Factor 5 Ds* are simple, not complex, allowing you to take the reins to achieve being powerful in your purpose. Remember that things do not need to be complicated to work. Independent thinkers understand that when something is too complicated, it can be discouraging. Discouragement leads to delay, which results in deviating from your plan.

You are destined for greatness and success. Before you were born, a special place of power was designed for you that only you can fulfill. Only you can do what you were especially made for. Someone else cannot meet or attain your destiny.

Have you ever failed at something? We all have. But sometimes, failing has nothing to do with incompetence or being unprepared. That failure could indicate that the assignment was not specifically for you.

Because you were in someone else's lane leading to their destiny, not yours, you had to be moved to the correct path to your destiny. Basically, you need to stay in your lane!

If you are feeling unfulfilled or powerless in your career or life, it could be because you are where you are not destined to be. If you have relinquished your power and someone else has determined your destiny, you are living another's dreams. No wonder you are unfulfilled and discontent. Do what has been gifted to *you*. The key to your success is *you*. Once you change your mind-set, you will turn your life and career goals around, moving from frustration to fulfillment.

With the elevation in your destiny comes increased responsibility. In fact, your place of destiny requires that you take more than just some responsibility. You must take all responsibility. Because your destiny is *yours*, you are the guardian of it, and have absolute authority over everything that comes with it. Fully understand that you are now responsible for the outcome of your life and career choices. If things don't go well, then you, the decision maker, are the leader. You are also the solution. Who else can solve the challenges in your life better than you? The old you authorized others to be your solution. But, the new *you* is responsible to be the problem solver.

The wonderful thing about problems is that a solution is to be found. The solution lies within you making the conscious decision to be responsible and putting in the work to bring your destiny into fruition. You are the leader of your life, and ultimately, you are always the problem solver. Responsibility means that the chains of the past are broken, and no one can control what you do or how you do it. No more blame game. No more giving control to others who dictate their ideals of who you should be. George Bernard Shaw, Nobel Prize winner, said it best: "We are made wise not by the recollection of our past, but by the responsibility of our future." Isn't it exciting that your future belongs to you?

Once you are under the influence of your own power and not another's, your eyes will be opened to view opportunities and possibilities in a different light. As a free-thinker, you don't plan as a pessimist, but as an optimist. A positive mind-set results in a more positive outcome.

Think back to a time when you were the passenger of your life. Contemplate that phase of your life for a moment. What emotions do those thoughts bring up for you? Maybe anger, frustration, vulnerability, or powerlessness. Focus on those feelings, going into deep thought. Compare those past feelings with feelings in your current position as the driver of your life. What new emotions do you feel? Do you feel joy, hope, or peace? Focus on these current feelings. Maybe you feel powerful now, instead of powerless. If you feel anxiety or fear in this fresh territory, you are not alone; however, while society may tell you this is normal, I encourage you to go against the grain and retain your power and control.

Moving forward also requires reflection. Reflect on the past to learn from it, but then focus on your future. I always encourage clients, groups, and audiences I work with to contemplate the past when stepping into this new area, as the driver. This allows you to compare past feelings with current feelings, emphasizing that to keep experiencing the new empowering feelings; you must continue to move forward. It is a motivator that has proven effective! Don't bring who you were into your new territory. You, as the driver, possess a superior energy, spirit, and attitude.

Your zeal to transform from dependence into freethinking shows enormous growth. You should be proud of yourself. As an independent thinker, you are enabled to have a more positive perspective as the leader of your own life. The more you approach situations with a positive and self-reliant attitude, the more you will not fear problems. You will see more solutions than complications. You are primed for increase in your personal and professional life. You are the driver! Be conscious and remember to unfailingly shift your mind-set into the power of positivity, staying aware that as the driver, you have unlimited possibilities.

QUESTIONS

1. What distractions have kept you from taking the action steps necessary to allow you to be the driver of your life?

2. What action(s) do you need to take to keep these distractions from hindering your growth and progress?

3. How will your life change for the better once these distractions are out of your life?

4. What will happen if these distractions stay in your life and you fail to become the driver of the life you were destined to have?

5. Write down an affirmation (it can be as long or short as you need) related to your being the driver of your life. Place this affirmation where you can see it. Recite it daily until it becomes part of your thinking.

CHAPTER 2
Discover Your "Why"

The Discovery Zone

When I discover who I am, I'll be free.

~Ralph Ellison, *Invisible Man*

CHAPTER 2
DISCOVER YOUR "WHY"

The Discovery Zone

Before you were born, or even a thought in your parents' minds, the universe had a special purpose designed especially for you. One of the most basic questions we all ask is, "Why am I here?" Where some people consider this question an unsolvable mystery, I know the answer is discoverable. Your purpose, however, remains hidden if *you* don't know where to explore. With deep thought, genuine commitment, and being honest and transparent with yourself, "The C Factor Discovery Zone" will guide you to *your* answer. Actually, the answer is already within you. The Discovery Zone just assists in uncovering the layers, leading you to reach your destiny.

No doubt you are asking, "What is my purpose? How do I discover my purpose?" These inquiries have many perplexed and frustrated, feeling as if they are wandering in a wilderness. These *wanderers* don't necessarily look frazzled or confused. In fact, many of them are polished, well-spoken, and successful individuals who are making six and seven figures in their high-powered positions. But, fortune and materialism does not equal happiness; neither does it mean they are living in their purpose.

One of the greatest discoveries you will ever make is to find out who you were born to be. Your *Discovery Zone* may even reveal to you that you have numerous purposes. Bishop T.D. Jakes, the senior pastor of The Potter's House, a global humanitarian organization, is a celebrated visionary. Being a proactive thinker, he says, "We allow people to put a 'period' where I believe God put a 'comma.' God put a seed in all of us. I believe that a forest can grow out of that one seed—not just one tree."

The *Discovery Zone* requires you to uncover the reason for your existence. Everyone, and I mean everyone, was purposefully placed on the planet for a purpose. When you unearth what that is, an entirely new world will open up for you. The *Discovery Zone's* revelation will provide absolute clarity on the direction for your life and why your life is important for the universe. Businessman and philanthropist W. Clement Stone believed that living out your purpose leads to success: "Definiteness of purpose is the starting point of all achievement." The shift that you are about to experience has tremendous success coming your way, in your personal life and your career.

It is not by happenstance that you are in a certain place at a specific moment in your life. Neither is it luck or coincidence. There was an appointment for you to be here in this space, at this present time. This appointment leads you to *your Discovery Zone*. Discovery is made possible only through meaningful query in which you are honest with yourself. There is no pass or fail, no right and wrong answers. There is no need to study, as your experiences and background will help you address questions that will break down the wall, divulging to you *your* direction.

The C Factor Discovery Zone Query

Are you ready? Be excited, for your discovery begins now!

What is missing from your life?

When trying to understand what's missing from your life, you need to begin looking within yourself. Do you consistently desire something? That indicates a high probability that the answer may lie there. Paying attention to this desire will help you to uncover that missing element. Feelings of emptiness may be affecting not only your personal life, but your professional life, as well. If you ever feel desolate, this is a revelation that a vital piece of the puzzle of your life is missing.

These are deep issues that require you to not only discover what is missing, but also *why* it is missing. Why is an element, or elements, missing in your life? Honestly addressing the *why* may be hard to face, because the responsibility is ultimately yours. Anything that is missing in your life is because you have allowed it. You are the *why*, not your family or others who have influenced your life. But, take heart! Whatever is missing can be found. Those burning desires within you do not have to remain desires. Turn your aspirations into realities; therefore, creating success.

What do you value most?

Your purpose is linked to what you value. What is important to you and what you hold in the highest regard is a definite clue leading you to your destiny. Value is subjective and varies from person to person. Time, love, peace, family, spirituality, and recognition are a few examples of what one may value. Think wholeheartedly about what is truly important to *you*. "You must look within for value, but must look beyond for perspective," said Denis E. Waitley, American motivational speaker and writer.

Before you determine what you value, above all else, consider how much you value yourself. It seems like an awkward question, but how much is in your vault? Your gifts, talents, and skills all have worth—you have worth. Many people forget they are of value. Having self-worth is not arrogance or imperiousness, for that is thinking too highly of yourself by demeaning others. Instead, self-worth is a characteristic of being human and made in the image of God, so you should be at the top of your highest-regard list. The higher your self-worth, the better able you are to prioritize other things.

What activities motivate you to go above and beyond?

Though we all have responsibilities and jobs, some people undertake them with more eagerness and exuberance than others. What tasks do you perform to the highest standard of excellence? More important, do you accomplish these duties without being asked? There is a difference between fulfilling responsibilities on purpose versus on a plea. Another way to ask this is what tasks or jobs would you do, whether or not you are paid? Your answer is a great identifier of your definite purpose and destiny. Think about when you are in your zone, using your unique abilities, techniques, and expertise to accomplish something. Being in your true space, the passing of time seems not to register. Your energy level stays strong, because of excitement of working your passion. Media mogul Oprah Winfrey is a crusader of encouraging people to live in their passion and purpose: "Passion is energy. Feel the power that comes from focusing on what excites you." I am a firm believer that what excites you will elevate you. What gives you that unusual energy of excitement? Whatever it is for *you*, follow that energy. This vitality will attract unlimited possibilities to you that will lead you to the highest elevation for your life.

How do you want your life to look and feel like every day?

Though simplistic, this question perplexes many people. Knowing that you don't want your future to look and feel like it does today is a step in the right direction. Not knowing exactly what your purpose is, you might feel a bit confused or be filled with doubt and fear. Don't let these emotions take up space in your life, cluttering your mind and soul. Letting them remain could drive you farther from your destiny.

Start answering this question by listing whatever elements you don't enjoy about your life. Then, list what you do want in your life. Don't rush this step. After you have finished your list, begin creating a strategy that will make your desired life a reality. Because you have a champion's mind-set, your imagination and potential are limitless. Think about and picture what you want your life to look and feel like. This is your design for success. Envision it. Visualize your unlimited possibilities. Making them an actuality puts you in your zone, where you are on your way to great gain.

When you are operating in your definite purpose, you will experience absolute contentment. The life you want, you can have.

What do you dream or think about continually?

Your creative power lies in the subliminal. Those subconscious thoughts may help lead you to your definitive purpose. For too long, the label *daydreamer* has had a negative connotation—someone who is unable to focus and may be lazy or unintelligent. However, I say dream, dream often, and, most importantly, dream on purpose. Independent thinking and dreaming is a prerequisite for achievement.

Without dreaming where would you be? Dreams are the bridge between you and your destiny. Dreams are the underpinning to your opulence. Your dreams provide hope, opening doors to the start of your victory and euphoria. Dreams have the ability to take you from where you are to where you aspire to be. Lailah Gifty Akita is a Ghanaian and founder of *Smart Youth Volunteers Foundation*. Her perspective on dreams is simple: "You can go as far as you dream, think, and imagine." Wherever your thoughts lead you, your purpose is not far behind.

Unlimited possibilities are preceded by how extensive your dreams are and how consistently you dream. Visions bring value to your life. Those dreams and thoughts are the sparks that fuel your determination.

If you no longer worked for someone else, how would you spend your time? What types of people would you surround yourself with?

Some synonyms of *work* are labor and chore. That's pretty bleak, right? If no one has told you, allow me: you do not have to work a nine-to-five job and just survive.

Do any of the following statements apply to you?

- I don't like my boss's management style.
- I hate my toxic work environment.
- I feel like my life is out of my control.
- I do not have control over my environment and who is part of it.

If even one statement describes you, maybe it's time to consider entrepreneurship, which allows absolute freedom and control of not only your job, but also all of your life. Being in control of your destiny, you have the ability to create your own space and determine who should and, more importantly, should *not* be in it. However, in whatever you do, whether as an entrepreneur or an employee, do it with excellence, always striving to reach the highest level of quality and your highest potential.

If you are not content working for someone else, imagine what you would do every day. If you did not have to work for someone else, who would you surround yourself with daily? Did you catch the words *have to* in the previous sentence? You could say that you don't have to do anything. You do not have to work for someone else. You do not have to work in a virulent environment. But, if you want to thrive, you do have to decide that you want more and then act on your goals and dreams.

Maybe, I'm speaking to your spirit. If so, then good. This is what the *Discovery Zone* is all about. If your spirit is stirred, now is the time for you to move forward to receive your unlimited possibilities that are waiting on your horizon.

What would you like people's perceptions of you to be regarding your purpose?

How do you want people to see you, as you fulfill your purpose? This is not in any way asking you to look to others for validation. But, the truth is that you make an impression on everyone you come into contact with. You leave your mark on every task you complete in your purpose. If you are the executive director of a nonprofit, the CEO of a Fortune 500 company, or an entrepreneur, you are making an impression in how you lead. Living out the plan for your life, you are serving others. Successful people are aware that their work is a kind of service. Living out your destiny with an attitude of serving with excellence puts your life into great perspective.

What impact can you make in your industry, as you live in your purpose? Our purpose is never about ourselves. It is not a selfish pursuit, but a selfless one. We were each given certain gifts and talents, and these special qualities are a great responsibility not to be wasted.

Remember that those whom you serve keep you successful, and reputation is everything. Several profitable enterprises have made their start through word of mouth. This is why the "six degrees of separation" theory is so true. How many times have you run into someone who knows someone who knows you? You can't argue with this theory that in this world, we are separated from others by six links. Therefore, those who are independent thinkers and successful understand the importance of reputation, always performing at a stellar status versus subpar. Warren Buffett, American business magnate, investor, and philanthropist, is considered one of the most successful investors in the world and has spoken on reputation: "It takes twenty years to build a reputation and five minutes to ruin it. If you think about that, you'll do things differently." It is important to consider the impression you leave, while walking in your purpose. Your reputation can precede you, opening doors or closing them.

ic*Looking back, are you where you thought you would be today?*

It is not uncommon for people to question their purpose and destiny. Living the same life day after day leads to months, or even years of a prosaic cycle. People don't necessarily work in a specific job or career for so long because they enjoy it. Oftentimes, it's simply a matter of habit. Some people have become numb to their daily routines, not even thinking about the monotony, but simply following their well-established rut, day in and day out.

Be honest with yourself: Are you just existing and not really living? I don't care how much money you make or what your title is, not fulfilling your purpose leaves you poor in spirit. Prosperity comes with purpose, so start living in yours. If you are not where you want to be, then stop wishing for it and start working on it.

This phase of the *Discovery Zone* is reflection without regret. Regrets take you away from your destiny, not toward it. If you are not where you want to be, don't regret it. Own that you are where you are in life, because of the choices you have made. But, don't stay there. Start today making choices that will lead you to your purpose and to your destiny. Create a blueprint to move on from your present situation.

Not being content or at peace should be enough motivation to start pursuing your destiny. This *Discovery Zone* can help you on the journey to encountering your purposeful place.

Now What?

Congratulations! You made it through the *Discovery Zone*. Now what? Discovering your route is just the beginning. Now that you know your path, the *C Factor* takes you through five life-changing steps to help guide you down your path and into your purpose.

Step 1: Get Rid of Your Baggage

Don't bring old baggage into your new territory. Make "Out with the old, in with the new" your mantra, as you walk into your definitive purpose. Those old characteristics that you allowed to control and trap you should be a thing of the past. That includes people, old ways of thinking, and adverse habits that held you back. Think about this: if these old things never helped you discover your purpose and move forward, why would you want to hang on to them? Admittedly, some of those things feel "safe" and a measure of comfort is found in the familiar, but, again, if they didn't help you move forward in life, then they are old worn-out baggage that holds you back. Being uncomfortable is part of the process toward your purpose.

Step 2: Make an Agreement

The agreement you're about to make is with yourself. Write a paragraph or two stating your purpose and that you promise to live in it. Believe this agreement with yourself as an affirmation. Recite this promise daily until it is deeply rooted within you, so that you can recite it by heart. It needs to become second nature to you.

Though this is an agreement involving only you, it means that your commitment has consequences if it is broken. Not keeping the promise to yourself to live in your purpose will send you back into complacency. This affirmation helps you stay committed to your progressive process.

Step 3: Make Your Dreams Action Steps

Transferring your dreams from your mind to paper will make them more obtainable for you. Your thoughts need to be written down, and then put into action. This is your plan for success. You should accomplish something from your plan every day, which will take you to higher levels in your personal life and career. The bigger you dream, the better the list, and the more you can accomplish.

Visualization has value, so use that to increase in every area of your life. A heightened thought process will also raise the bar on the schedule of your goals. You will always be adding to your plans, because you will never stop dreaming. Dreams and actions go hand in hand. After you dream and write down items to reflect on, take action on them. If you don't, you will just have dreams.

Step 4: Prepare for Your Purpose

After you set your agenda, prepare for your purpose. How will you turn those action steps into success?

Like anything in life, preparation is required, so prepare for your success. Expectations should be accompanied with the appropriate preparation. Should your purpose require additional education, plan how you will get and pay for the education. If your destiny is to be an entrepreneur and expand with a storefront, research areas that would be an ideal location for your specific type of business. For your business goals, preparation is vital for obtaining investors and securing clientele. The more strategic measures you take in the beginning will help to create that flourishing future you are dreaming of.

Step 5: Go Get It!

While dreams build hope, there comes a time when you have to actually put feet to your planned actions. Dreams don't come true unless you take action on them. Your strategy will take your purpose from paper and preparation into reality. There is no other way for your purpose to be realized without working your strategy. No shortcuts. No procrastination—those things are old baggage. This is where the hard but rewarding work starts. Success is waiting for you on the other side. You are in an exciting time now, about to grab hold of everything that is destined for you. Now go and get it! Make it happen!

These five steps are all it takes to possess the significant life-change that awaits you. Once you dedicate yourself to the process, put in the work, and follow through, you will soon be in possession of the things you have dreamed about. Things that held you back in the past should be left in the past. Commit to the action steps, prepare for success, and start making moves. Remember, your thoughts don't move off of the paper until you move.

It's great to plan for the now, but it's necessary to make additional goals for the future. Create short-term goals, but think long-term. Victors and champions do not just think about today and tomorrow; they consider where they want to be years from now. An example of a short-term goal is hiring a consultant to create an innovative marketing plan for your company. The long-term goal would be to increase revenue by fifty percent by the end of the current year. People who are effective in business and have a productive life are ever goal-setting. They see beyond the present, always wanting to stay ahead.

Successful people living in their purpose know what they are going after and why it is important for them to obtain it. One of the greatest tragedies in life is not when you aim high and miss the mark, but aiming too low with barely a mark in sight. The higher your thinking, the higher you achieve. But if you aim low, well, you know how it ends. You will never win with ground-level thinking. A basic life doesn't just happen to someone. That individual made a choice to settle. Choosing to simply "squeak by" is a defeatist attitude. Winners and high-level thinkers never feel defeated. No matter the challenges or difficulties, they never feel like throwing in the towel. You get what you give. When you put extensive dreams and thoughts out into the universe, you get a substantial return. The dreams you nurture and build today are what you become tomorrow.

Your Definite Purpose

The *Discovery Zone* is where you can have your "aha moment," when you know why you were placed on this planet. Following are a few invaluable advantages of your definite purpose:

A Definite Purpose Is a Magnet, Attracting the Resources You Desire and Need

When you know the direction you are traveling in and for what reason, your mind shifts to that purpose and considers everything you need to live in it. It is true that what you reflect on is what you attract. Previously, your feelings of confusion, self-doubt, fear, and frustration were sending out mixed messages to the universe. However, now your energy has changed. Your effervescence is enthusiastic, organically attracting all that is necessary for you to successfully and fully live in your purpose.

A Definite Purpose Creates a Courageous Spirit

Now that you know what you are here to do, clarity has awakened in you something powerful! Successful people are courageous, living out their dreams and destiny with boldness and confidence. *Courage* is defined as "the ability to do something that frightens one."[1] Courage and fear cannot coexist within you, because they contradict each other. No matter the hurdles and challenges you face along the way, your courage does not let you stop. Instead, it compels you to progress until you claim your prize.

A Definite Purpose Makes You More Decisive

Those who are purpose-driven have the ability to make quick and effective decisions. With a clear roadmap that leads to your target, you don't have to guess what you should do while moving forward. Self-doubt is a thing of the past, making sound judgment and certainty your compass leading you into the future. You are not dependent on others as you were before, but you are making decisions with total confidence and independence. This is where you are sure to shine as an independent thinker.

A Definite Purpose Increases Your Faith and Belief

In my life, living on purpose, I have had to lean on my faith in God. When things don't go quite as planned (and that will happen), God is my universe and my purpose-provider. My total dependence on Him allows me to make it through the tough terrain and come out on top. Faith is something successful people find necessary to function. In fact, it's their nucleus. Unshakable faith keeps them grounded and focused, knowing that they will overcome difficulties. Whatever your faith, you need something that will keep you at peace and with a positive outlook when encountering frustrations and complications.

A Definite Purpose Has You Living the Life of Your Dreams

Believe me when I say that you can have absolutely anything you desire if you dream and follow up your thoughts with action. "Keep your dreams alive. Understand that to achieve anything requires faith and belief in yourself as well as your vision, hard work, determination, and dedication. Remember, all things are possible for those who believe," said Gail Devers, two-time Olympic champion. Your life of purpose will have you thinking limitless, instead of limited. In your life, you will continually aim higher as you achieve goals, surpassing previous goals, and breaking barriers. No one and nothing can put you in a box or make you think you can't prosper. Isn't that amazing? What you thought you couldn't do before; you now know you can do. With this newfound courage, you will be living a life without limits!

To have a life filled with unlimited possibilities, you have to believe that you are here for a particular and special purpose. You were born for a reason. You do have a definite purpose. If you have not discovered what your purpose is, you do not need to feel like you are hopelessly wandering. The universe has not forgotten about you. Discover what you were born to be. This is what the *Discovery Zone* is all about.

Oftentimes, your purpose is right in front of you, but you can't see it or hear that inner voice, because of distractions. Distractions are hindrances and dream killers, so remove them. Life can be hectic at times, so de-clutter your mind of those interruptions. Feeling stuck is another hindrance. You may be in a rut, but that doesn't mean you're stuck in it or have to stay there. You have the power to get yourself out of any situation. Don't let your present state fool you into thinking you don't have an amazing future.

Knowing your purpose emboldens you to reach the highest heights. Successful people believe that something better is always waiting for them. They don't wait for opportunities to come to them. They go out and grab everything that has their name on it. It doesn't matter how much they have or have not yet achieved, they know that there is always something greater.

If someone offered you a priceless gift, wouldn't you reach out and accept it? Of course! Think of your purpose as a perfectly wrapped package. This purpose, or destiny, is a gift with your name on it. What is especially made for you, no one can take from you. And no one can fulfill what you have been purposed for. Discover your gift that is waiting for you.

Do not let your present state keep you pessimistic. Before you can believe that you can have more, you must believe that you deserve more. No more excuses. Start executing your plan for your purpose. No more distractions. Start to live in your destiny today. It's time to discover the magnitude of your absolute destiny and the unlimited possibilities accompanying it.

QUESTIONS

1. What baggage has been holding you back from moving forward?

2. What is missing from your life?

3. How would having these missing elements improve and add value to your life?

4. If you don't take action to bring these missing elements into your life, how will your life be?

5. How do you want your daily life to look and feel like?

6. What action steps can you take to realize your desires?

CHAPTER 3
Develop the Art of Self-Discipline

How Bad Do You Want It?

Virtues are the fruit of self-discipline and do not drop from heaven as does rain or snow.

~Zen Saying

CHAPTER 3
DEVELOP THE ART OF SELF-DISCIPLINE

How Bad Do You Want It?

Procrastination is the dilemma of self-discipline. Tomorrow. Next week. Next month. Next year. Uttering, even thinking these words is absolute poison to your success. Procrastination is a dream killer. The funny thing is that it creeps up on you, subtly and without notice, until one day you wake up to the brutal fact that you are in the exact same position when you first started discovering your destiny. Playing the waiting game, procrastinating, and being indecisive have contributed to your being where you are in life at this very moment.

Much like the snowball effect, procrastination is a growth that starts from something small. It then becomes larger, ever increasing in size and all the while deterring you from living in your destiny. One hour of procrastination can lead to losing excessive amount of precious time. How often have you asked yourself, "Where has the time gone?" Time is one of the most precious commodities on earth. Time is like nothing else. When it is gone, you cannot get it back.

In the business world, time is equal to capital: "Time is money." Allowing time to slip through your fingers can cost you your financial well-being. That hour or two you did not manage well may have cost connections to potential clients and thousands of dollars. Your business depends on the time you put into its economic growth. The pace you choose to be productive determines how prosperous you become.

How do you spend your time? Honestly assess the number of hours you wasted this week. Ten hours? Three hours? Wasting even one hour is excessive. Successful people view and spend time distinctly from the rest of the world. They don't view time lost as just wasted. Their heightened level of thinking evaluates how much closer they would be to their goals and success if they had been more strategic in using their time. Your relentless pursuit of your purpose will not leave any room to waste time.

Being casual about life and your time will result in disappointments, lack of fulfillment, unmet goals, and a retreat from your destiny. Bruce Lee is acclaimed not only for his skill in martial arts, but also for his philosophic intellect. He sees respect of time as an authentic love for life: "If you love life, don't waste time, for time is what life is made up of." Those with a heightened awareness of their purpose and destiny want to live and thrive in it every second of every moment. Devaluing time devalues your life and purpose.

View your time as you do relationships. If you are with someone who doesn't respect and appreciate you, you lose respect and appreciation for that person. Eventually, the relationship will end. Don't lie to time. Make your schedule and stick to it. If you plan to work on a project from 1 p.m. to 2 p.m., stay true to that. Once you make your schedule, you are committing not only to yourself, but to time that will perform an action. When you don't fulfill that covenant, it's a broken promise. Again, you have a relationship with your time, so treasure it. Treat it as you would someone you value and love. If you are good to time, then time will be good to you.

Progressive people have a special attachment to time, something like a bond. Be dedicated to time, taking a vow to respect, cherish, and value it. American businessman and philanthropist Jon Huntsman Sr. said it best, "Decide who you are and what your goals entail—then go for the roses. Life has little regard for those who waste time."

Oftentimes, procrastination and the lack of self-discipline rule when you are in a place of *have to* and not *want to*. One of Oprah Winfrey's creeds is "Do what you have to do until you can do what you really want to do." Discipline is the bridge between goals and accomplishments. Getting to the other side of procrastination when you are in the *have-to* phase will get you to the life you want. You cannot skip this step. Push through this phase to live full in your destiny and purpose. How well you manage your time in this stage will determine your level of success and personal fulfillment.

When you have wasted a chunk of time—even a day or more—don't you feel a sense of guilt and maybe even failure? However, when you use your time wisely, you have a sense of satisfaction. Making good use of your time brings you steps closer to living the life you desire. Start viewing time as successful people do. They use time to plan, prepare, learn, evaluate, and move forward. All of that requires self-discipline. Without it, you will be lost to your destiny.

Let's say that things are good in your life. You are happy in your business and in your purpose. That's great, but as an ambitious person, you know something more is *always* waiting to be achieved. You can reach higher levels. Constantly developing and growing should be on your mind. Don't stop at good. How many exceptionally successful people were satisfied with average? Actually, that statement is an oxymoron. You can be average or exceptionally successful, but not both.

Greater fulfillment requires greater achievement. Your present achievements should not halt your future fulfillment. They should be a springboard toward permanent gratification of fully living in your destiny and purpose. Going from good to great takes time and robust self-discipline. It necessitates using time to fulfill short-term goals, as well as long-term goals.

Procrastination may also be a sign of fear. Believe it or not, some people would rather stay in the uneventful "safe" pool, than risk unknown waters. They are afraid to delve into new discoveries. I tell these people that if they don't start moving toward their destiny, a year from now, they will be wondering what might have been had they not given in to their fears. The ripples and waves of the waters of life may look uncertain, but you just have to jump in. When you do, you will not sink, but swim. Like Nike says, "Just Do It!"

The key to overcoming procrastination is to stop thinking about what *might* go wrong and just start working your plan—and don't look back. Think where you will be five years from now, as you use self-discipline to keep you on track toward your ultimate destiny. American entrepreneur, author, and motivational speaker Jim Rohn said, "Discipline weighs ounces while regret weighs tons." Self-discipline brings dreams into reality, while procrastination leads to a life of regrets.

Beware of These Distractions

Have you allowed distractions to deter you from your destiny? Be honest. Distractions are a death trap for self-discipline, subtly stealing time away and keeping you from reaching your destiny.

Others' Opinions

Being in your purposeful territory, you may feel like a newbie on the block and experience a bit of insecurity and uncertainty. This is absolutely normal. Seeking the opinions of others is a conventional human behavior, but not being cautious of the source of the opinion can be a distraction to your destiny. Those who genuinely love you may tell you what you want to hear. Though they mean well, they can do more harm than good. Also, an individual's opinion may be limited. He or she may not be qualified to offer the kind of advice you need. If others' thinking is limited in their own lives, they will place limits on your life. This is why accomplished individuals urge you to surround yourself with like-minded people.

When getting advice regarding your goals and dreams, seek the viewpoints of those who have successfully traveled the road you are currently on and who are greatly achieved in their field or industry. Who better to support you, encourage you, and share lessons learned on your journey, than those who have been where you are? This type of mentorship is invaluable to your succeeding in your purpose.

The Power of Social Media

Comparing your business and success to another's is like comparing apples with oranges. Social media has great power, enabling you to market yourself to a wider audience and thus gaining maximum brand exposure. The other side of social media is that it has the potential to create personal dissatisfaction. Seeing another's post about an accolade or new client can create feelings of inferiority. However, you don't know the story or struggle behind the post. This may be that individual's first award, or the client could be their first new client after several months. Also, social media posts are easily fabricated. As the saying goes, "People are not all who they post to be."

Instead of focusing on another's lane, stay in your own, keeping focused on your purpose. Yes, countless others are doing work similar to yours, but comparisons are never necessary, as there is only one you. Comparison always leads to dissatisfaction. Don't devalue yourself based on another's success. Your quality of life and level of achievement in your destiny is all determined by your belief in yourself.

Your Comfort Zone

Over the past few years, several established retail businesses that have been around for decades are closing their doors. Why is this happening? Rather than staying current with trends and customers' buying habits, they continued doing business as they always have. Why is your business no longer growing? Have you stayed in your comfort zone, rather than keeping current on changes and trends in your field, as well as your customers' needs and habits? What worked when you started your business ten years ago will not work today. Industries are ever evolving, and you should evolve with yours, or you will be left behind.

Never stop learning and always seek growth. Being lulled into your comfort zone with the "this is what worked in the past" distracts you. You then miss out on opportunities not only to gain new customers, but to keep your current ones. "Out with the old, in with the new" rings true in your purpose, as well.

Disorganization

Being disorganized is a disaster and a distraction in your destiny. If I may be blunt, it is a chaotic mess. Your project, company, or business will never reach its peak if it lacks organization, physically and administratively. For example, if your physical space is disorganized, everything you do takes longer to accomplish. Before you can work on Project A, you have to move clutter out of your way. Likewise, if you lack administrative organization, some tasks will be overlooked, while others will be done several times. In both cases, disorganization is costing time and money.

Organization is a measure of a business's health. If organization is not your strength, you owe it to yourself to bring in a professional organizer. An organized business is efficient and productive, which translates into profit and growth. If you want the most out of your day, year, and purpose, be habitual in getting and staying organized.

Downtime

Earlier, I talked about not wasting time and not letting distractions pull you off course. Now, I need to add that you need a healthy balance between work and downtime. That's right, nothing is wrong with a little downtime. In fact, downtime can actually boost your productivity and satisfaction.

It is unreasonable to work 24/7/365. That is unhealthy, and there's more to living your destiny than just work. Family responsibilities, other relationships, and community involvement are all important elements of a balanced life. Then, too, downtime from work allows you to refresh and restore your energy, making you happier and more content in living out your purpose.

One caveat to downtime is to be vigilant that it doesn't devolve into wasting time in front of the T.V. or doing endless searches on the internet. Never leave your self-discipline at the door when you take a little time off, for you'll need it to keep you from succumbing to distractions that too easily can slip in unnoticed.

Trade in Procrastination for Self-Discipline

Let's say you are done with procrastinating and are ready to learn self-discipline. But how do you make such a drastic change? Following are several tips to help you develop the necessary skill of self-discipline.

Stop Making Excuses

If you say that self-discipline is hard, I agree. However, what I can't agree with are excuses for a lack of self-discipline. "This is just the way I am," is the most common excuse I hear. If you accept that, then also accept that your life will stay the same.

Become familiar with the phrase "Excuses are inexcusable." Write it down and deposit it in your memory bank. Anytime you are tempted to make an excuse for your lack of self-discipline, remember this quote. These three little words will save you from a downfall in your destiny.

We have astounding power to impact our lives—positively or negatively, depending on how we use that power. You have the power to change your attitude from giving excuses to learning self-disciple, which leads to a life of excellence. It all starts with your decision to use your power to move your life forward into your destiny.

Just Decide

Ending procrastination and developing self-discipline starts with a conscious decision to change. If you don't choose to be self-disciplined, then you cannot transition to a more successful life. It's not just a cliché; it is true that you must change your mind-set to create greater for your life. You have to decide you want better. You have to decide you are tired of stagnation and subpar, or average. You have to decide that you want everything that has your name on it. Most importantly, you need to believe that you deserve better.

Life is all about decisions. From the time we get up in the morning to the time we go to bed, we make decisions. When you woke up this morning, you may have decided to hit the snooze button, opting for a few more minutes of sleep. You make decisions every moment of the day that will ultimately affect your quality of life, so decide wisely. Choosing to be self-disciplined means that you are no longer delaying the prosperous purpose meant for you.

Be Mindful of Your Words and Thoughts

Your thoughts create your habits, and your habits create your future. Whatever you think and speak, corresponding actions will follow. To succeed, you must be self-disciplined about your thought pattern and language, because whatever you speak and focus on becomes a reality. We oftentimes become the words we speak and the thoughts we meditate upon. If you want your dreams to become actuality, then think them, speak them, and, most importantly, live them. In every thought you manifest, in every word you utter, and in every action you take, it should be intentional and purpose-driven. Speaking in the affirmative has a domino effect impacting your entire life for the better. Speak, "I am self-disciplined in the area of [fill in with whatever is true or what you want to be true]." Keep repeating this until your words and actions become habit. Robert Schuller was an American Christian televangelist, pastor, motivational speaker, and author. "The only place where your dream becomes impossible is in your own thinking" were his words and belief regarding dreams and mind-set. Whatever thoughts are counter-productive to your success should be changed to productive thoughts. Your self-limiting beliefs will have you living a life of limited possibilities as opposed to unlimited. Any self-doubt is not reality and is based on false information. Change any illusions in your mind that are in opposition of the words *can do*.

Sacrifice

You must be willing to pay the price of living a self-disciplined life. You first have to do what you don't want to do, so you can enjoy the life you deeply desire. When you procrastinate, life is comfortable and predictable. But when you decide to become self-disciplined, your sacrifice to get out of your comfort zone will give you serious success.

Looking at it from a different perspective, you are actually sacrificing your success if you are not self-disciplined. Blood, sweat, and tears are partners with self-discipline. Late nights, early mornings, and pushing though the hard times are all a part of your transformation to a self-disciplined individual. Paying the price will help you maintain focus and secure your future. You must be willing to forsake your present comfort to pursue what will bring you future fulfillment.

Be Committed

Committed means wholehearted dedication and loyalty to a cause, activity, or job. You must be single-mindedly loyal to your cause, or to your purpose. Half-hearted commitment equals being only half fulfilled in your life. You cannot experience full success with a halfhearted commitment. Imagine receiving only half of what you are destined for, because you were not fully committed. You want all of what is purposed for you, not half. But, if you put in fifty percent effort, then that is what you will receive. Your level of work and commitment determines what you receive. This process requires you to make a promise to yourself that you will stay loyal to the necessary action steps to be effective. When you are not wholeheartedly committed to your purpose, the only one you are hurting is yourself. Breaking your commitment contract hurts you and your progress. When the poison of procrastination creeps into your commitment, it can delay, or even deny, your destiny.

Stay Ready

Actor Will Smith said that if you always stay ready, you don't need to get ready. Athletes are always in training mode, knowing that they need to be prepared when called to play in the game. In the game of life, you also must be *training* at all times, ready for anything that comes your way. You should expect great opportunities and events while living in your destiny, so never procrastinate preparing yourself. Strategic management of your time is part of your conditioning. Preparing is non-stop, as each step up you take and each level you rise to takes an elevated level of preparation. Are you staying ready to be purposely placed into your destiny?

Strategize Your Day

What daily practices are not necessary to your flourishing? What are those things you do that are of no benefit to your progression? Maybe it's time to stop doing them.

Life seems to be all about making lists. You might have twenty items on your to-do list today, but which items are most essential? What tasks contribute to your overall success?

I don't have a to-do list; rather, I have a "Success List." With each duty I tackle, I know I am doing it with purpose and it is furthering my success. My daily motivating mantra is "I define how my day is going to go. I control my day. My day will not control me." Also, I have five categories (A through E) on my daily list for success:

- A— must be done
- B—has to be done
- C—do when I can
- D—delegate
- E—eliminate

When you categorize tasks, you feel less stressed and are more productive, focusing on duties that are relevant to your success. Be strategic with your list for success, asking yourself what thing(s) will create revenue. Many people are so focused on making lists for every little thing (e.g., grocery shopping, pick up dry cleaning), but regarding your purpose, prioritize what generates income, gives you increase, and brings opportunities to get to the next stage of winning. Say *no* to what does not contribute to your productivity, and say *yes* to those activities that help take you to greatness.

Be Intentional and Balanced

To be intentional requires self-discipline. In everything you do, do it with intent. This includes having a healthy balance in your life. When you are at work, be committed to your work, projects, and clients. It is not healthy to work non-stop, so don't work when you are at home. When you are at home, be dedicated to your loved ones, your family time, and your household responsibilities.

Also, be committed to your sleep, to being well-rested. Granted, great responsibilities might cause a sleepless night now and then. But, when you have the proper amount of sleep, you will be more productive. Trying to function on three or four hours of sleep a night will cause you to crash during the day and keep you from being your best. If you can, get six to eight hours of sleep each night and don't feel guilty about it.

UNLIMITED POSSIBILITIES

Develop Yourself

It doesn't matter who you are, everyone has twenty-four hours each day. What you have done with your daily allotment is how you will be remembered. Don't be remembered for money or materialism but instead, for making a positive impact in your sphere of influence. Remember, your purpose is never for yourself. Develop yourself, so you can be a great benefit to others.

Whatever your process is for self-development, be disciplined in it. For example, I follow a daily agenda that is the foundation for my evolution. I begin my day focusing on my spiritual, mental, and physical wellness with meditation and fitness. Then, I turn my attention to goals. I write down five business goals and five personal goals, then visualize these goals. I should mention that these goals are affirmations. My goals are not written as wants, but as things I visualize as already having. It's important that you think, speak, and act as if you already possess your desires. The most important thing in my personal development is being faithful to continually study my area of expertise.

Never stop learning. As your field of business changes, make sure you are current with trends—even ahead of them. You cannot make an impact in your purpose without vast knowledge.

I also want to encourage you to be disciplined in your everyday ordinary actions. For example, I never leave the house, until my bed is made a certain way. Being disciplined in minor things will pave the way for you to be that much more developed on a higher level. Develop yourself daily.

Self-discipline is a requirement to developing yourself. It is not easy, for if it were, everyone would be a master at it. Self-discipline forces you to do what you don't want to do. Self-discipline kicks in when it's most convenient for you. There is no shortage of discipline regarding leisure activities and your comfort zone. The difficulty comes in when you experience fear, self-doubt, or maybe even unwillingness. You can be selective in your self-discipline, which is not necessarily a bad thing. However, I encourage you to maintain your self-discipline. When the going gets difficult, or you're out of your comfort zone, don't fight self-control—align yourself with it, for you need it most when life is uncomfortable.

It is a process to foster this willpower. But, once you master this elevating exercise, you will witness the opening of countless doors to unlimited possibilities. The procedure for mastering self-control is as important as the promise of your prosperity. But don't miss the task, because like anything in life, it is necessary to grow, move forward, and advance. To accomplish this, you have to follow definite steps.

Also, though my method is universal and applies to all people, your undertaking will be distinct from another's. Just like destinies differ, so must the actions for each of us to arrive in our greatness.

Procrastination and self-discipline cannot coexist. One will always dominate in their tug-of-war in your life. Turn procrastination into self-discipline by committing to your purpose, your goals, and yourself. The excitement of being self-disciplined should have you eager and ready to achieve. Distractions and time killers become a thing of the past, because you will not authorize them to come into your present and rob your future. You are now productive and ready to perform to your best potential.

One of the most asked questions on earth is "What if?" What if you would have worked harder? What if you would have been more disciplined? What if you would have truly lived in your complete destiny? What if you would not have let distractions get in the way? Don't put yourself in a place where you look back over your life with regret. Being self-disciplined, you will have no regrets and no *what-ifs*.

Becoming self-disciplined requires sincere effort. This very moment in your life is critical, as it is your time to make a decision. Determine to use your power of mastering self-discipline to move you forward. Your destiny depends upon it.

QUESTIONS

1. How has a lack of self-discipline affected your life?

2. What distractions keep you from being self-disciplined?

3. What can you do to ensure that these distractions will no longer hinder your self-discipline?

4. How will you create a success list, as opposed to a to-do list?

5. What are five personal and five professional goals that you need more self-discipline to achieve?

CHAPTER 4
Visualization

Can You See It?

In order to carry a positive action, we must develop here a positive vision.

~Dalai Lama

CHAPTER 4
VISUALIZATION

Can You See It?

• • • • • • • • • • • • • •

"Imagination is everything. It is the preview of life's coming attractions," said Albert Einstein. The word *imagine* is a verb meaning "a mental image or concept, or to suppose or assume."[1] Whatever you visualize for your life, your thoughts suppose or assume it; therefore, turning it into actuality. Your mind is the landscape architect for your viability. However you use your creative consciousness to visualize, determines how far you will go in your destiny, direction, and attainments. Unlimited possibilities don't just fall into your lap. You attract them through your thought patterns.

Visualization is a powerful tool. Where many fail to move forward and do not live their lives to the highest level is not because of their inability to use this capacity, but it is their unwillingness to use it. If you feel powerless and are not living up to your full potential to be powerful in your purpose, it is because you have chosen not to use your potential. I will never accept the excuse that one cannot use his power when it is that he has chosen not to use his full abilities.

For various reasons, some people are reluctant to succeed and live in their purpose. Let me share the top four rationales that contribute to living a limited life.

Background

Those who grew up in an environment of poverty, had no example of what success is, or were told that they would never make anything of themselves are at risk of living a limited life. However, individuals who were reared in a more stable environment with encouragement and had all of their needs met have a higher probability of living a limitless life.

Many people are living in a box, because that is the life they were exposed to while growing up. It is a type of comfort zone. The difficulty is to see anything more than what they know, or are familiar with. Statistics have shown that your background and family upbringing influence your actions, thought patterns, and decisions. However, numerous individuals limit themselves, giving the excuse that they are a product of an unfavorable upbringing. But, this is not so. Although it's true that as children, they had no control over their environments or family situations, but as adults, they have the ability to choose what kind of life they will live going forward. For every study done determining the future of those who grew up in an adverse environment, I will give you countless stories of those who beat the odds. In fact, I am one of those people. Growing up in poverty, we didn't have our wants met, and many times, our needs went unmet. But, something inside of me wouldn't let me believe that this was all that life had to offer. The environment you grew up in does not have to define who you are or determine what you will achieve.

See beyond the known; take a risk stepping into the unknown. Your ability to visualize will allow you to see beyond your background.

Comfort Zone

Who doesn't want to be comfortable? Having a life of ease is something all of us want. However, the easy life is not realistic if you want to advance to the next level. This is why so many people settle for *what is*, instead of succeeding at *what can be*.

There are no shortcuts to achievement. It comes with sacrifices, hard work, and taking risks. Your dreams are put in danger when you become too comfortable with your present state, not fully living in your purpose and fate. Remaining in your comfort zone will make you sell out your goals and ambitions. Saying it plainly, comfort zones will have you living a life that is confined. What differentiates the limited from the limitless is staying with what is known, as opposed to moving into the unknown, which is a superior and fulfilling life. It doesn't matter if you are just starting out on pursuing your destiny or if you have been working at it for a few years: just because you have earned some accolades and made great accomplishments doesn't mean that you are done. Don't get too comfortable in your success. You can always take your business, project, or organization higher. If you remain in your comfort zone after achieving some success, it won't be long until your competitors surpass you. Don't opt for complacency. To be truly victorious and living unlimited possibilities, break that bondage called your *comfort zone*.

Habit

Doing something long enough can become a habit. However, some habits are a hindrance to your becoming a champion. Some people say that habits are hard to break, and that's true. However, it is not impossible.

For our purposes, I will address habits from the perspective of them keeping you from progressing into your destiny. For example, let's say Joan goes to work every day at the same job she's had for several years. She doesn't hate her job, but she doesn't necessarily love it either. She clocks in at 9:00 a.m., does what she's supposed to, and waits for the clock to strike 5:00 p.m., so she can leave. She continues her mundane, passionless job and lives a monotonous life every day. She doesn't even think about it anymore, and just lives out of habit. Does this describe you? Or is a spirit of the unknown trying to pull you away from your habit-job, calling you to a bigger and better life? Have you been fighting it? Well, this is your wake-up call! Habits can be broken. It's up to you to answer the call for your life to truly start living without limits.

Fear

We will talk more about fear later in the chapter, but the number one reason for remaining restricted in existence is fear. As I've spoken to groups and individuals around the world, I have heard more times than I can count, "What if I fail?" My response, "Well, what if you do?" Why would you allow fear to make you a failure when you haven't even begun? On your path to greatness, you will encounter disappointments and challenges, but with a changed mind-set, you can view these with a sense of optimism.

The obstacles and complications you encounter in your pursuit don't make you a failure; they are just lessons directing you where you need to be on your journey. You are a failure, however, when you let fear control you, so that you never attempt to win. Winners face fears. Don't think that those who have achieved success have never been fearful. That is just not so. We all have fears and reservations, but the difference between achievers and others is that achievers fight through fears. Difficulties give us wisdom and make us stronger. You cannot know the strength you have without taking a few curveballs. To be a winner, you must face your fear and push through self-doubt. It all starts with your mind-set. You are stronger than you think.

If you have let any of the above excuses hinder you from even trying to reach the top, I want to encourage you that you can overcome these challenges. It doesn't matter your background or the length of time you have been doing something out of habit. If you don't like where you are, use your inspiration to change your position. There is extreme value in your visualization.

When your logic is raised, visualization can create mental pictures that help you understand that these thoughts are absolutely attainable. When you see others achieving superlative success, it is partially because of their intelligence, but it's also due in large measure to their courage to envision beyond the normal. Your mind is the seed that influences how extensive or modest your dreams advance.

There is no secret to the power of visualization. The universe does not have a limited number of individuals who have been selected to succeed. No other way to say it but that if you have not succeeded, it is because you have not utilized your power. Deep within each of us is a purposeful power to take us to a more prosperous existence. Being a spectator, you will never hone this power. Being complacent will never reveal the strength of your competence. Once you allow your mind to unleash extraordinary thoughts, your life will have no limits. Limitless is what you will become, but it starts in your mind.

UNLIMITED POSSIBILITIES

Even though your dreams have not yet become a reality, firmly believing that one day they will be is all about faith. Faith gives you the strength to believe the unbelievable, unimaginable, and what some consider undoable. Where some have to see it to believe it, successful people's faith gives them the ability to believe it before it is in their grasp. Because of faith, you can be relentless in pursuing your passion. When things become difficult, your faith is tested. No matter the struggles, challenges, or setbacks, faithful individuals have the tenacity to push through pain and into a life of plenty. Keeping your faith is not always easy, but it is essential to your journey.

Faith, like anything in life you want to perfect, takes ceaseless dedication. Whether it is prayer, meditation, or something else that allows you time with a higher power, that bond and relationship must stay strong and unbreakable to be effective in tough times. My ability to pour into you through this book is all due to my past experiences and the faith that allowed me to endure.

My faith in God helped me to attain unlimited possibilities. Faith allows you to believe that you will receive your desires. You don't have to actually possess it in the present to believe that it will be yours in the future. When you have faith and then put that faith into action, you will be unstoppable. Write down in a journal your desires. Create a vision board. Write your wants on index cards and place them around the house where you can easily see them. Your spiritual life will also help you in this process. Faith allows you to believe, even if present circumstances are difficult. At my lowest points in life, my faith brought me through. You have to have one-hundred percent unwavering belief that you will succeed. You must have a conviction in your spirit that these things you cannot see will become your reality.

Attached to faith is gratitude. When I speak on action, being grateful is part of it. You must have an attitude of gratitude though you have not received your thoughts and desires. Also, you have to be thankful for what you have, while you are waiting on the unlimited possibilities. Keep a grateful spirit and let your actions line up with that thankfulness.

Don't choose to be excellent when you have arrived at a level ten; be excellent, while you are at level one. Don't ever accept mediocrity in minor things. Practice excellence in ordinary things. Be excellent on all levels. When I started my first business, barely making ends meet, I made sure my customer service was stellar. Being faithful where you are will open doors for your unlimited possibilities.

Things we don't even realize can impact our ability to visualize. Be very cautious of what you are taking into your mind and spirit. What is the first thing you do in the morning? If it's watching the news, then that can plant only negativity into your thoughts. Starting the day off hearing about robberies and murders is not productive to your visualization. Take in only positive vibes to properly visualize. Be mindful of music. Even sad love songs can make you sad, or even depressed. Be conscious of everything you are taking in, understanding that what comes in will come out. What works for me is starting my day off with inspirational reads, books, and music. Beginning your day with inspirational influences will prime you for a day of progress.

Visualization is not something you do every now and then or once a week when you feel like it. You need to visualize throughout the day and continuously act on what you see in your mind's eye. I spend a set amount of time daily to visualize goals. Some people visualize first thing in the morning and then before bed. If you find it hard to visualize, it could be because you are too distracted. Each of us has responsibilities and obligations; however, don't let those tasks keep you too distracted to focus on your future. Don't become too distracted with the things going on with this world that are insignificant and irrelevant to your destiny.

The process of visualizing for a more successful life is not mastered overnight. Past experiences as well as stresses of everyday life and other responsibilities can make it hard to see a more advantageous existence beyond the present. However, your perfection of a positive outlook can make or break your dreams. Choose to let them make your dreams. Visualization can be very effective, but it can also be extremely ineffective, putting you in a state of pessimism. Instead of talking yourself into opportunities, erroneous visualizing can cause you to subconsciously talk yourself out of opportunities.

Think back to when you felt an unexplainable force pulling you away from prosperity. Maybe you didn't rent that available space for your business. Possibly, you failed to apply for a promotion. Did you pass up an investment opportunity that you now regret? Why did you let these opportunities for elevation pass you by? We talked about fear being a reason for one living a limited life. Fear can pull us back from accepting opportunities.

Visualization can bring out fear if not done properly. Dangerous situations or pain, whether real or imaginary, can cause fear. What are you afraid of? What is driving your imagination toward fear?

Successful people are not driven by fear, but by their faith in an awe-inspiring future. Individuals with a heightened sense of belief have trained their minds to automatically visualize their purpose, destiny, and victory. The phrase "Seeing is believing" is not in their vocabulary. They believe in their vision before they can see it in the physical realm. They can feel, touch, and taste their dreams coming into reality before they can hold them in their grasp. Until you displace the thought of having to see it before you believe it, fear will stay at the helm of your life.

How to Visualize

You may wonder how to visualize. Let's start with a little test as I call *The C Factor Visualization Test*. Don't be nervous. There is no pass or fail. This is to help you see the power that lies within your ability to visualize. This is where your faith and visualization are tested.

Go to a quiet place. It can be in your office on your lunch break or even in your car, as long as you can do this test where it is quiet and without any distractions. Close your eyes. Take a few deep breaths and just sit and clear your mind for a minute or two. No distractions and no background noise. You should be in total peace and serenity. What is something you have been envisioning and desperately want for your life, but have felt it is impossible to obtain? Focus on this for a moment. Imagine living in your element. What are you doing in it? Are you running your own successful business? Maybe, you are traveling the world. Whatever it is, how does it feel? What emotions are you experiencing, as you are visualizing? Living in your destiny should bring about good feelings. Hold on to this excitement; never let it go. With true concentration, conceive its possibility. Now, open your eyes and take a couple of deep breaths.

Until you master the art of effective visualization, in silence is one of the best ways you can gain results in the present. Once you become a master "visualizer," your abilities and thoughts won't be limited, as there will be no need to have a specific quiet space for you to conceptualize in. Very soon you will be able to visualize anywhere, any place, and at any given time.

How will your life change for the better if what you visualized becomes your reality? On the other hand, how will your life be if your focus remains on fear and you don't even attempt to make positive changes? If you want to achieve success, make your dreams and goals a reality, you must position your attitude always on your possibilities. It is doable to claim the victory you have been dreaming about. My continuous hope for you is that any fear that has occupied your thinking will be overridden by promising prospects for your future.

Effectively Visualize for Success

This brief exercise was just to get you started and the wheels turning. To be effective in transitioning expectation into existence, you must follow the process.

Control Your Thoughts

Oprah said it best: "If you want your life to be more rewarding, you have to change the way you think." Your mind is the director for your destiny. Thoughts create habits, and habits create the future. Depending on where your mind goes, you can enjoy slight or great gain. Unfavorable thoughts develop an objectionable outcome. Let's use this everyday example. When you spilled something, have you ever said to yourself, "Oh, how stupid!" You are talking to yourself with negative energy. Stay continually aware of your thoughts, controlling them, so that you think positively. Whenever you spill a glass of milk, keep a positive outlook. When you make a little blunder, say, "Oh well, let's deal with this then move on." Do you see the difference? The power of positive thinking is crucial for your future. Your inner dialogue will always determine the quality of your life.

Be Desperate

Where some say making decisions out of desperation can bring disaster, it is here that being desperate is an asset to accessing unlimited possibilities. How bad do you want to get out of that thankless job and be your own boss? How bad do you want the life you have always dreamed of? When you are desperate, you will not give a second thought to the sacrifices you must make to get to your destination. You willingly make them.

Let me state a caveat. Please don't think I'm saying that you are to be desperate, so that you become ruthless and literally take out your competition. You don't have to lie, cheat, or steal to gain success in your purpose. Your purpose is specific for you, so if things are meant for you, you will receive them.

Be desperate to reach your dreams to the point of making great sacrifices, while keeping your integrity. Your desperation should drive you to sacrifice that vacation to invest in your business. You should be so driven to your unlimited possibilities that you will sacrifice sleep to work on that goal for an extra hour. Be persistent in your pursuit of prosperity, understanding that you have nowhere to go but up. Don't stop until you arrive.

Cut the Clutter

You cannot think and be productive in a cluttered place. Just like you do spring cleaning at home, you must also do some mental spring cleaning. When your power or psyche is cluttered, you cannot move forward. No doubt, it has been long overdue to rid your mind of that mess and those distractions that have been keeping you from operating in superior territory. Throw out the self-doubt. Toss away the dismay and the procrastination.

In addition, don't take on too many projects at once. That is one of the biggest mistakes in goal setting. Prioritize what is most important to your unlimited possibilities. What will result in profits? What will get you closer to achievement? These are questions to ask yourself when making your success list. Everything is not important. Being realistic about your goals will help you simplify. And once you de-clutter, these blockers are considered nonreturnable and unrecyclable. De-cluttering is a determinant in your advancement. Clean out your space for more clarity!

Be Thankful and Reflect

Don't let impatience interfere with progress. Always remain in a state of genuine gratefulness. Be thankful before you achieve and receive. Not to be confused with complacency, keep an attitude of gratitude for where you currently are. The journey to your destiny is filled with invaluable learning experiences that will keep you from falling, as you are elevated. "An attitude of gratitude" is a simple, but straightforward truth.

Reflect on where you were last year or even last month. Aren't you farther along than you were a couple months ago? Celebrate your progress made thus far and applaud what you will receive. Do you see faith at work in this? You will be able to celebrate what you have not yet received, because you know that unlimited possibilities are in your future. Reflect on the positives, and the growth and wisdom, you received along the way. Your present place is only temporary. Focus on your permanent place in whatever field you are working.

Change Your Circle

You are definitely known by the community you keep. Motivational speaker Jim Rohn pronounced that we are the average of the five people with whom we spend the most time. This relates to the law of averages, which says that the result of any given position will be the average of all outcomes. Community greatly influences our thought patterns and even decisions. Your circle of friends influences you. Successful people surround themselves with successful people. Why? Like-minded individuals have an energy that attracts them to one another. Now, this is not to say that you look down on others whose mind-set differs from yours. It is just that, as you grow as a person, you want more for your life. Your walk is different and so are your conversations. You need positive people in your space on your journey. These positive people are not *yes-men*, for weak people agree with everything you do. You want people with strength in your immediate group who will give you necessary constructive criticism. Research shows that we are more impacted by environment, than we commonly believe. It is natural to want to be with people who share your values and vision. Change your circle, and you will change your life.

Scare Yourself

The imagination can conjure unlimited possibilities. One phrase I use to encourage the audiences I speak to is "Go big or go home." That's right! Go big with your thoughts and desires. With this planet so substantial, why is your creative consciousness not matching the extent of the wonderful world we live in? Enormous advancement is coming your way, but you have to think bigger. It all starts with a thought. Your imagination should take you to crazy, larger-than-life notions that scare you they're so wonderful. I'm not talking fear. Maybe, instead of "scare you," I should say *shock you*—in a good way. Have you ever had a thought so outlandish that you laughed at the idea and wondered, "Can I actually do this?" That little shock was a result of your new way of processing in your purpose. Your mind was experiencing a little bolt, as it transformed to a more heightened mental procedure. Your new way of imagining should take you out of your comfort zone and scare you into success.

Possess Clarity

If you don't have clarity on your purpose, you cannot move forward. The eyes are the gateway to our souls. What are you seeing with your inner eyes? I pose this question to those I coach: "You can look, but are truly seeing?" Some cannot see and that is why they are stuck on a merry-go-round, while attempting to live another's purpose. This happens quite often. When you don't know your purpose, you look at someone else who is successful and try to live as they do, thinking it will work for you, too. However, their destiny is not yours, and trying to live theirs is like living life on a hamster wheel. You must be clear about what *you* want in life. The *Discovery Zone* is beneficial in finding clarity. Once you have clarity, then the process can begin.

Have Faith

I hope you see that having faith is of great importance. Too many people don't even get to square one, because they don't believe. Some days will be tough, as you journey to the top. You may face opposition and even rejection; however, your faith will keep you looking toward your future, rather than any failure or disappointment. Faith kicks in when the world seems to be kicking you. Faith is the energy to keep you pushing through. One of the most amazing things about faith is that fear cannot reside with it. It has to be one or the other, and the choice is all yours. Fear will cause you to fail, but faith allows you to fulfill your specially designed destiny. Your mind, body, and soul are strengthened with faith. When you are feeling weak and like you can't continue, that spark of faith will reignite your burning desire and keep you moving into your destiny. Also, faith keeps you humble, grounded, and appreciative when you receive. In those times of seeming failure, your faith allows you to grow and learn, affording you the ability to be the effective leader necessary to lead your organization or company. When disappointments don't immediately disappear, neither should your faith.

Practice Makes Perfect

Remember the *C Factor Visualization Test* we did earlier? Continue to do this exercise, until it becomes second nature. You have received confirmation of your divine purpose; now, your thoughts need to line up. Practicing with an eye on perfection takes place during your regular meditation time, which increases your motivation. Regardless of your natural talents and abilities, you must practice them to hone them. Great people practice their crafts daily. To succeed in the game of life, this visualization test is a part of your practice method, so practice, practice, and practice, until you become a master visualizer, then practice some more. Continue to perfect your purpose.

What do you visualize for yourself? What is the life you want? In your grasp and within reach is all that you want and more. The great thing about the universe is that it will lead you to wherever you imagine.

UNLIMITED POSSIBILITIES

Your imagination and thoughts can lead you to a dynamic life, fulfilling dreams and goals that you never thought possible. Can you see it? If you can see it, then you need to believe it, which will result in your achieving it. Don't place any limitations on yourself. Don't let others place restraints on you, either. Your mind knows no limitations. Visualizing can bring victory.

After effectual visualization, it's time to move forward: make a plan and start taking immediate action. Things just don't happen by coincidence or luck. You have to make them happen. Your imagination and plans must eventually come off of the paper and activity has to follow. It may begin with a thought, but in the next phase, you must push the plan into motion. "Vision without action is merely a dream. Action without vision just passes the time. Vision with action can change the world," said bestselling author Joel A. Barker. Start to change the world with your vision followed by actions.

QUESTIONS

1. What has caused your lack of faith that your goals and dreams can be reality?

2. Visualize your top three goals and dreams for your personal and professional life. What emotions do you feel envisioning these things for your life?

3. What fear(s) has been holding you back from receiving your unlimited possibilities?

4. What steps can you take to push through your fear(s)?

5. Look at your circle. Do you have five people in your immediate circle who are a positive influence on your progression in your purpose?

CHAPTER 5
SET YOUR STRATEGY

What's Your Plan?

Your life can't go according to plan if you have no plan.

~Author Unknown

It's not the plan that is important, it's the planning.

~Graeme Edwards

CHAPTER 5
SET YOUR STRATEGY

What's Your Plan?

• • • • • • • • • • • • •

I wholeheartedly agree with Benjamin Franklin who said, "If you fail to plan, you are planning to fail." Now that you have masterfully maneuvered through your *Discovery Zone*, gained clarification on your purpose and destiny, changed your mind-set from fear to faith, your life is about to get very real. Why? Because now that you've made your plan for success, it is time to start the work to move to the next level. No more writing things down, and no more thinking things through. You are ready for your next step, an exciting step, into the unfamiliar.

Don't let the unfamiliar trigger fear, for this is an extremely exhilarating time for you. Victors and champions don't get fretful, but they effectively and unhesitatingly work their plans. Because you are a champion as well, approach your plan with focus and confidence. Think about it this way: being swift while executing your strategy means you are taking action that will get you to the life you are destined for. Nowhere in life can one be successful *without* a plan. It is necessary to transition visions, thoughts, and dreams onto paper and into a plan, which determines the actions to create your desired achievements. It's great to have a plan, but without action, nothing happens. Successful people unfailingly apply a strategy that sets their plans into motion, making fortune a reality. Designing and working your plan will make you triumphant in possessing the unlimited possibilities of your purpose!

It is important to understand that everyone has a strategy for their lives, whether by design or by default. Designing your destiny results in winning, whereas lack of purposely pursuing any plan will result in failure—a lack of success. Making it plain, design determines your destiny and default determines your defeat. Why would you not want to design your plan for a more magnificent life? Your personal strategy is behind every success or failure you encounter. Don't let fear talk you out of creating your strategy to realize the unlimited possibilities you deserve. Always choose design over default.

Being strategic is carefully designing your plan that will serve a particular purpose. First, consider your purpose and goals. Next, and most important, decide how you will accomplish them. *Your plan is all about the why, how, and what.* Why do you want the unlimited possibilities? How will you arrive at your unlimited possibilities? What steps will you take to realize your unlimited possibilities?

Leaving your life to mere happenstance won't help you excel. If you want a breakthrough, then don't wish for it, hope for it, or sit around waiting for it; make it happen!

Once you achieve a taste of success along the road to your purpose, expect change. (Never expect "chance.") Change is good. This is especially true regarding your destiny. Do not get too comfortable and complacent in your process, as it may be necessary to make adjustments to your plan from time to time. Your plan doesn't have to be set in concrete, and it should welcome modifications over the course of this journey.

If you have been implementing your strategy for some time with no results, then it is unwise to continue with that same strategy. If your plan isn't working as you want it to, a correction is in order. Don't ever be embarrassed to admit you need to make a change in your design or strategy. The way to your revolution is through your ability and willingness to revise your efforts. To be blunt, if what you have been doing is not working, then just stop doing it. Do something new and do more of what is working. Awaken each day committed to your process, but be open to change.

Unless you consistently work your plan, you are simply left with a nice to-do list. Your mission is not only to make a plan, but to be a skillful planner. The key to your prosperous purpose is dependent upon your successful system and your master-planner mind-set. The clear passage from your present to where you aspire to be is determined by your strategy. Champions strategically develop their plans, because this is what launches them to a successful destination. Do you want to do just well, or do you want to abundantly exceed expectations? The choice is solely yours. It is in your hands to form and implement the proper action steps.

So what's your plan?

Law of Preparation

The Law of Preparation is simple: never *not* be prepared. Maybe you were expecting me to say something more poetic. Though the message is simple, it's loud and clear. To be triumphant, you should not *get* ready for opportunities; rather, you should always *be* ready to receive and walk into possibilities of greatness as soon as they present themselves. Nothing comes to fruition without preparation. Without proper planning and preparation, it is likely you will not obtain the highest level of fulfillment you desire. *The Law of Preparation* is necessary, as it is all about arrangement in your favor. It benefits you in several ways. Let's look a few.

It Provides a Roadmap to Your Destination

How can you get where you are going if you have no address or directions to follow? You can't. Baseball legend Yogi Berra was quoted as saying, "If you don't know where you are going, you'll end up someplace else." Not planning will have you in a state of utter confusion, wandering around in the wilderness. I cannot stress enough that plans direct your path. Notions remain nothings, unless you write them out.

You can write out your plan using pen and paper. If you prefer, your laptop might be your choice. Whatever works best for you to achieve greatness, transfer your ideas from your mind into visual form, so you can see them, reflect on them, and act on them. What's important is that your proposal be clear, concise, and detailed.

Additionally, don't worry about your plan being too simplistic. That's better than it being overly complicated. Remember, it is your plan, so design it with *you* in mind. Just make sure that your procedure takes you from where you are to where you want to go.

It Prepares You for Challenges

The truth is that though your design gives you clear direction, it will not keep obstacles out of your way. No one is promised a perfect life. Everyone, and I don't care where they are now in life, has experienced any number of challenges.

More important than the challenges is how you deal with the inevitable stresses. Being realistic doesn't mean that you will always have a positive attitude and outlook. It just means that you don't need to fear the unknown, because you have properly planned for it.

Where some say you don't need a Plan B, I highly disagree. Successful people, and especially those who are effective leaders, not only have Plans A and B, they also have Plans C through Z. Think about it for a moment. Earlier, we talked about change and how it is beneficial to implement it on your path. Changes are certain in life. So, don't think that having backup plans is a negative attitude. It is just that in order to adapt, you have to be in the frame of mind to expect the unpredictable every now and then, which means you'll have wisely prepared for the unforeseen occurrence.

With that being said, I don't want you to be focused on the unexpected, as that could push you into a fearful frame of mind. As opposed to being fixated on the unexpected, concentrate instead on the unlimited possibilities that are within your grasp. Being a victor, not a victim, your backup plans are tools to help you through the challenges you may face. If you don't create a design for the unexpected, then when they hit, they will most definitely break you. Your ability to adapt will make you wiser and stronger in dealing with any difficulties. Because you have a master plan that is clear and includes your Plan A, as well as alternate plans, you will be able to face challenges and walk through them victoriously. Change is inevitable and constant. With skillful planning, you can address any change with absolute confidence, as you continue to pursue greatness.

It Provides You with Patience

The Law of Preparation provides you with patience. When things come easy, you rarely appreciate them. Pursuing your unlimited possibilities, instead of having them handed to you, puts more value to them once you possess them. Working for your goals and pushing through with blood, sweat, and tears, *the Law of Preparation* gives you a heightened sense of gratitude and pleasure for your purpose, in the end. When I speak to groups around the world, I ask them what they cherish in their lives. The common response is that they cherish most what they worked for. Think about something you truly cherish in your life. Don't you hold in high regard those things you invested time and effort into?

Your willingness to win will bring about patience and a greater sense of appreciation for your achievements. It also allows you to understand that you did not reach your level of success alone. Patience allows you to throw ego out the door, keeping you mindful that no one has created great things alone. God, and those who supported you along the way, deserve credit. Patience does not let you forget that. Patience also keeps you sensitive to the fact that your purpose is not about you. We all are gifted with special purposes for the benefit of others and not ourselves.

Patience brings an increased sense of selflessness. You are stronger than you think, but without patience, you may never know just how strong. With each obstacle you overcome, your level of patience increases. Your patience will show you what you are made of. Pretty soon, you will not view patience as "the waiting game," but as a process preparing you for your purpose. Therefore, when things don't go according to your plan, the unforeseen elements won't deter you. Trust that you will make it through difficulties better than when you first encountered them.

Applying patience on your journey will give you a much greater respect for your purpose. Without patience, you will disregard moving toward your destiny. You were birthed for an amazing purpose, but you will have to do some work along the way. Basically, if you don't work for your purpose, you won't appreciate it, thus possibly abusing it by not using it as it was originally intended. Patience is necessary for your development to fully live responsibly in your purpose.

It Provides You with an Amazing Outcome

If you want a prodigious outcome for your future, then engage in the *Law of Preparation*. Alan Lakein, acclaimed author on personal time management, said, "Planning is bringing the future into the present, so that you can do something about it now." Ruminate on that for a moment.

Earlier, we spoke on patience being part of the process. However, the future is brought into the present through your master planning. Accurate forethought opens the door for you to begin the process to receive your unlimited possibilities. Not only are you writing your own future, but you are bringing it into existence. The outcome is dependent upon how bad you want those unlimited possibilities. How great your desire to win is based upon how large your dreams are. How bright do you want your future to be? *The Law of Preparation* gives you permission to be the preparer and creator of your life. So, why create an average outcome when you can design an awesome and amazing one? I assume you want the latter. Those with a high sense of achievement always want the best life possible, filled with the most prosperous outcome.

Your mind is a wondrous tool. The more you conceptualize and desire for unlimited possibilities, you increase the probability that they will come into your possession. The *Law of Preparation* is your permission to design and establish your majesty.

The Law of Preparation should have your wheels turning now. As you plan, a magnetic force is bringing you and your future unlimited probabilities together. You attract what you desire and believe you are destined for. Use your thoughts like seeds to plant your dynamic design. Water them with action steps to germinate your greatness.

A Master Planner

The difference between a plan and a master plan is actually quite simple. An average plan comes from an average mind-set. An average plan might include a vague idea of what age you want to retire, vacation to the Caribbean, or to have your house paid off at a certain date. The plan might even include a couple of strategies to achieve your goals. But, it remains vague and not much action is applied to it. A master plan is an entirely different animal. The master plan is clear and concise. It states specific action steps that will take you to your destiny, and it includes a timeline. Your master plan includes, among other things, a picture of the group of people you will surround yourself with who will help you toward your goal. A master plan is monumental; therefore, giving you more substantial success.

Creating a master plan makes you a master planner. Your master plan means the difference between having a good life and a great life. Master planning means your level of thinking is higher than average individuals. It doesn't mean you are better than the average person; it just means your thinking is different. You won't settle for the white picket fence. Instead, you aspire for more than average. You want everything on the outside of the fence. Your dreams are not fenced in. Being an independent thinker, you don't follow what others say success is. Instead, you create your own paradigm through your limitless ability to imagine unlimited possibilities.

Decide right now that you want a better life. Decide, at this very moment, that you want more than what you have already achieved. Choose never to settle. Make your decision and then move forward, master planner, to create the life you have longed for.

Have a Clear and Concise Vision

High achievers do not create a plan, until their vision is clear. You cannot formulate a plan if you don't know what you want to accomplish or what you want your future to be. Vision and victory go hand in hand.

Your vision must be clear, so you can fully reach your potential. Champions don't base their plans on what they think their vision is, but on what they one-hundred percent know it is. An unclear vision makes for an unclear plan. Without a clear vision, you will create unnecessary frustration. You could be consistently confused and hit brick walls, because your design may not necessarily be in line with your purpose. If your vision is even a little unclear, rely on your faith, meditation, experiences, or other methods to help you think through, until you achieve clarity. Wherever you want to go in the future depends upon your vision.

You can dream big, but make sure your vision is not complicated, thus confusing even you as to what you are working toward. Complicated cannot provide you with an effective plan. Unless you have a concise and intelligible vision, the master plan cannot follow. Be clear in order to be outstanding.

Be Obsessed

Be obsessed, but in the healthy sense. According to *Psychology Today*, non-clinical *obsession* refers to a disproportionate or unusual focus on something.[1] It simply means people pay more attention to something, than most others do. In all my years in business and coaching, I have not encountered any individual with stellar levels of success who do not exercise a certain degree of obsessiveness. "To do anything to a high level, it has to be total obsession," said Conor Anthony McGregor, Irish professional mixed-martial artist and professional boxer. Are you working daily on your aspirations? Are you focused on finding your unlimited possibilities in your purpose? To be profitable, you should be obsessed. There is nothing wrong with being obsessed (non-clinically, of course) with your purpose and success. Whatever you consistently think about, you can achieve it if you believe it. Having a healthy passion for your purpose will give you security and plenty.

Understand the Difference between a Plan and Planning

"Plans are nothing; planning is everything," explained Dwight D. Eisenhower, the thirty-fourth president of the United States. *Plans* and *planning* are often used interchangeably, but they have different, though related, meanings. Plans are documented programs of action. Plans can change or be altered.

Planning is specific for particular fields and sequential action steps to set goals. When you think planning, think about taking action. Your planning allows you to make things happen. Planning helps to keep you on track by evaluating trends and looking at other relevant details that will move you increasingly closer to achieving your dreams.

When you hear *nothing in life is guaranteed*, don't believe it. In fact, throw any cliché out the window that limits you or tells you things are impossible. Now, let's be realistic. Life can throw you curveballs, but look at those times with a positive perspective. Any complications that occur, your action steps give you the ability to rise above, helping to guarantee your success and to increase your chances of winning. Your steps bring your destiny out of the documentation phase.

Be Extremely Disciplined

Discipline, and I mean extreme discipline, makes for a wondrous destiny. Crush those goals with discipline. Triumphant people use self-discipline to keep them focused on their futures and clearing the clutter in their minds that can distract them from their purpose. The difference between a planner and a master planner is that a master planner is self-disciplined. Ultimately, self-discipline determines whether or not you will attain your destiny.

Discipline takes strength, willpower, and determination. Distractions, such as negative people, self-doubt, and unacceptable bad habits can be very destructive to your process. Whatever those things are that draw your attention away from your goals and cause you to lose focus, requires extreme discipline to get rid of them or to establish safeguards in your life, so that they don't control you. Do whatever you must do to remain on track. Discipline means you may need to turn off the cell phone or mobile device, keep distance between you and certain individuals, or even change your environment. American entrepreneur, speaker, and author Jim Rohn said this about discipline: "Discipline is the bridge between goals and accomplishment." How high you achieve in your destiny is dependent upon the level of your discipline. Be disciplined and be exceptional.

Set Deadlines and Value Time

Successful people not only have goals, but also realistic deadlines by which their goals should be achieved. If you don't have a deadline, you lessen your chances of fulfilling your objectives. "Deadlines are your lifeline," as the familiar phrase goes. Setting a date indicates valuing time and future achievements.

A deadline is not just about you. Your clients, employees, and business, or company, are all depending on you. Security and organization are protected with deadlines, without which your progress can be delayed. Tasks and projects can go undone for days, weeks, and maybe even months or years. Your path to greatness requires deadlines. Master planners invariably establish a timeframe for each and every aim. Without specific deadlines, your goals are at risk of just taking up space on paper and not fulfilling your purpose. You don't want to simply wish that you would have achieved, regretting the precious time you wasted. "We must all suffer one of two things: the pain of discipline or the pain of regret or disappointment" is another fitting quote from Jim Rohn. Respect your goals. Respect your future. Respect your time. Create deadlines!

Have a Mastermind Alliance

Speaking on mastermind alliances, Jonathan M. Tisch, chairman and CEO of Lowes Hotels, said, "You're not going to be great at everything. Surround yourself with people that can compliment you so you can work together and then everybody can be successful." In the business world, it has been said, "Teamwork makes the dream work." The same is true for you. Your dream will not work if you do not have the right team. No one ever makes it to the top on their own.

Be extremely selective when putting together your mastermind alliance, for they influence your decisions. These people become a reflection of not only who you are, but where you are going. Your mastermind alliance should include individuals who are committed to the cause, putting their time and energy into your initiatives. Choose trustworthy people to be on your team who have the same high level of integrity and character, as they do experience.

Form your team of masters to help you achieve greatness. This group you create has to be made up of like-minded individuals who have a high level of expertise in their field. You cannot and will not know everything. In whatever area of your enterprise you are not highly skilled in, bring in individuals with that kind of experience.

Every facet of your organization should run like a well-oiled machine, and these leaders you have chosen should have not only the proficiency, but the valuable leadership and management experience to lead their respective teams. Also, there should be no conflict of interest among your team members. One of the most important traits when choosing your mastermind alliance is the ability to contribute to the bottom line, keeping you in the black. In whatever assignment each member of your alliance performs, they should be working toward increasing profits and expanding your brand.

Your selected group of individuals must believe in your vision and implement your strategies, so you can win—and not just you, but also your team. An effective leader of a mastermind alliance is not selfish, but embodies a *true* team spirit. Your team should feel empowered bringing their special gifts and talents to the table. They, too, will benefit from their efforts. Successful people have a pattern of winning, because of their formation of an energetic environment in which *everyone* feels they are a part of something great.

Make a Wise Master Plan

Planning is critical to your future, so plan wisely. You are the master designer for your life. Don't put limits on your imagination, for it is the gateway to how far you can go. Dream big, plan big, and produce big. Your thoughts of where you can go in life should scare you a little. So, shock yourself with thoughts of how high you can achieve. When your dreams and goals make you laugh and you think you're a little crazy that usually means those are things you need to work toward. If your dreams don't scare you, then keep dreaming. Ellen Johnson Sirleaf is often referred to as the "Iron Lady." She was Africa's first elected female head of state. As a history maker, she said, "The size of your dreams must always exceed your current capacity to achieve them. If your dreams do not scare you, they are not big enough."

There is no room for playing it safe when it comes to your purpose and master plan. *Master* is the key word. You are the master of your fate, so if you are in absolute and complete control of your thoughts, let your imagination take you to great heights. Really think about this for a moment. If you can have any life and obtain anything you want, wouldn't you go for it? Of course, you would! So, don't think small. Be a visionary leader in your purpose. Strive to make history. Go for gold. You are in control and are the driving force of the establishment of your life.

Now What?

After you plan, what's next? Take *serious* action. Plans and goals don't move, unless you do. Achievement is a direct result of your deeds. How many times do you hear people wish others good luck? They mean well, but the truth is that there is no such thing as luck when it comes to *real* success. Roman philosopher Seneca once said, "Luck is what happens when preparation meets opportunity." This is a reminder to move with your master plan, so that you create your own "luck." Anything in life worth having doesn't come without its share of sacrifices and hard work. It's like I always say, "Earn it and enjoy it."

If you have built a successful business, that is great. But, how far can you take your business with expanding your brand or even rebranding? Will expanding your brand increase profits? Have you not yet followed your purpose and took that leap of faith to live your dreams? This is an absolutely amazing world with unlimited possibilities. No more excuses. Don't ever stop living life to the fullest. You are designed and intended to experience unlimited possibilities. I want you to believe it, but do you believe it? I can't want more for your life than you do. You will be left with regrets if you never live in your purpose. Don't wish. Do!

Many people create plans, but not master plans. This separates those high achievers from the rest. What is your plan or, should I say, your master plan? By now, you should have a keen awareness of the master planning process. You have it in you to be a master planner. In fact, you *are* a master planner with no limits as to how high you can achieve.

UNLIMITED POSSIBILITIES

This is a gentle reminder for you to consistently speak in the affirmative. The only limits that exist are those that you put on yourself. So, set out your winning master strategy, and make it happen. Design your plan for an eventful destiny.

QUESTIONS

1. What is the clear and concise vision for your life?

2. If you have a plan, what can you do to transform it into a master plan?

3. If you have not done so, start working on your master plan. What top three action steps can you take to achieve your goals?

4. What are the top elements of your master plan?

5. What challenges have you faced that if you'd have had a master plan, you would have been prepared to successfully push through?

6. Who is a part of your mastermind alliance?

CHAPTER 6
DEVELOP YOUR KNOWLEDGE & GIFTS

How Well Do You Know Your Craft?

Incredible change happens in your life when you decide to take control of what you do have power over instead of craving control over what you don't.

Steve Maraboli

CHAPTER 6
DEVELOP YOUR KNOWLEDGE & GIFTS

How Well Do You Know Your Craft?

Imagine a room of absolute elegance, immaculately decorated with an assortment of bright colored balloons—reds, purples, yellows . . . every exciting color under the rainbow. The decorative details include silver silk drapery embroidered with shimmering bronze threads. Champagne flows from gold-trimmed flutes. Tables draped in the finest linen display the richest and most delectable hors d'oeuvres one can imagine. The music is inspirational. The lighting is perfect. The mood is comfortably opulent. At the center of the room is a large candlelit table covered with superbly wrapped gifts in a variety of sizes. Each present is labeled with your name, transcribed in calligraphy. It is not your birthday, so what is the occasion?

No special event was necessary to gift you with a purpose. Actually, your gifts were predetermined before you were born. Your special combination of gifts and abilities are no one else's. A definition of *gift* is a "notable capacity, talent, or endowment."[1] Also, most importantly is that these gifts serve a purpose. You possess the power of these gifts for your destiny.

Notice that I said *gifts*, plural. We each have more than one gift, or what we might call talents or natural abilities. Gifts vary from individual to individual. Where some may have the gift of public speaking, others have the unchallenging ability to run an organization, build businesses, manage a team, and make profits. We know we are gifted with the power of supernatural superiority when we do certain things with ease and without any formal training. For example, those gifted with music have natural talent to quickly learn to play instruments, sometimes self-taught. Those who are gifted mechanically innately know how machines function.

However, just because you were given a talent doesn't mean you should not hone it or perfect it. Developing your gifts is a part of your great responsibility. The skills and knowledge you acquire through experience and education make your natural talent blossom into great ability, which unlocks the door to your unlimited possibilities.

Our gifts are not meant to be unused or to remain undeveloped at their lowest level—or even at an average level. Your gifts are to be improved and used at their highest level. In fact, that is why God gifted them to you. God knew you would treat these gifts with such high regard, that you would handle the great responsibility that comes with them, so He gave them to you. You must work on your talents *daily* to perfect them, so you can use them as they were intended. It is your responsibility to manage your abilities, and part of that means never being complacent.

Additionally, developing your knowledge and skills is crucial to your success. People who are masters at their gifts are never content with being *good enough* in their fields. These individuals strive to be expert leaders. You are already over the first hurdle with possession of your gifts, now it is time to advance them, to develop them, so that you become an expert in your field, which will bring you vast advantages.

For you to truly be an effectual leader in your field, and to aid your team and clientele, you must be highly knowledgeable and skilled in your line of work. Leaders who are strong, influential, and run their businesses well are also well-respected, because of their dedication to constantly developing themselves and their talents.

Let's take for example one who is gifted in business affairs. Imagine two businesspeople from the same background and with the same education. They started their businesses at the same time. Both businesses are in prime locations, but one business failed to make it past the one-year mark. How is it that all things being equal, one succeeded and the other did not? Luck! Luck! Luck! Everyone wants to talk about luck, but luck was not a factor. It all has to do with gaining knowledge in one's particular field and developing one's gift. Where some business owners fail within the first year is that they are operating just at the curve, rather than ahead of it. Having knowledge in all areas of your business is the foundation to your success.

In anything you do, make sure you are not just good, but always an expert. The business world is highly competitive. You must be on top of trends, client expectations, products, and more, or you will be out of business. Stand out from your competitors by becoming an authority. Many people start a project, organization, or business, because they are good at something. To be brutally honest, being good is not good enough. You should always strive not only to keep your spot, but to have the top spot by always increasing the knowledge and skills required of your industry. Then, people will come to you as opposed to your competition, because you have made yourself an expert with unique understanding and service they can receive nowhere else.

As an authority, you will attain a whole new level in your purpose. If you want to see how high you can go, aim for excellence. It is not necessarily those who have several degrees and have been in their craft for an impressive number of years who are the experts. It can be the one who came from poverty, didn't attend college, but learned and developed expert skills through experience, dedication to their gifts, and acumen. Anyone can be an expert if they put in the work. Don't be intimidated by degrees hanging on the wall or the accolades of others. You are a pro, too, but you have to believe it. It all starts with your mind-set. As I always say, "Believe it, and you become it." If you are not yet the pundit you would like to be in your purpose and calling, then start studying now to develop your skills and knowledge.

How to Develop Yourself as an Expert

Where some say *it is easier said than done*, don't believe that. It is actually easier done than just said when you take the proper steps and follow the process.

Study

We are typically encouraged not to reflect on the past, but to keep moving forward. But, when it comes to being an expert in your field, I encourage you to look back and evaluate events and trends in the past. Successful businessman Tom Hopkins is quoted as saying, "An expert is someone who knows a lot about the past." To be an authority in your field, you need not only to study the current industry trends, but also consider its history and those who came before you. Studying these things will help you avoid common mistakes, think creatively about your business, and keep your profits high and losses low.

Study people! School yourself on the characteristics of those who are where you aspire to be. The habits of the wealthy and successful differ from those who are just breaking even. Do a little comparison. Look at your practices compared with those who are acclaimed in your field and find the similarities and differences. What adjustments can you make in your life to better match these winning people? Your routine, from the moment you awaken in the morning to when you lay your head down to sleep at night, determines your destiny from this day forth.

Don't forget to study your competitors—what they're doing and why their practices are working where yours may not be. What procedures do they follow for their employees that are enticing yours to leave? Evaluate their methods against their successes and then determine what you need to adjust in your business practices.

Another characteristic of being an expert is that you never stop gaining understanding. Once you learn something, delve deeper. Don't just know something, but know the history behind it and why it works. Great leaders never have a spirit of *arrival*. They know that there is always something to learn about their ever-evolving fields. Your study habits will keep you from being blindsided by the constant changes in your industry. When you study, you become a pundit in your purpose and the master of your fate.

Practice

After you have gained greater knowledge of your industry and your competitors, put your knowledge into action, thus emerging as an expert leader in your field. "Observe, record, tabulate, communicate. Use your five senses. Learn to see, learn to hear, learn to feel, learn to smell, and know that by practice alone you can become expert," said William Osler, Canadian physician and one of the four founding professors of Johns Hopkins Hospital. Practice can eventually make perfect.

The application of your knowledge when you dive into deep waters of experiences will help you swim the waters of success. When it comes to your purpose and taking risks, dive in. On the other hand, sometimes to adequately be prepared in your purpose, it's absolutely alright for you to wade in the baby pool before going into the deep end. From your studies, you will know the correct approach for each situation.

Living in your purpose is a beautiful thing, but it will not always be free of challenges. I would be remiss as a business coach if I were to mislead you into thinking that everything, at all times, will be perfection. You can thoroughly enjoy your purpose, while also being aware of obstacles you will likely encounter. But, this is nothing to fear. In fact, this is what practicing is all about. How many teams that have won the Super Bowl did so without practice? Great performers never step onto the stage without practice and proper preparation. The same applies to you as you work out your destiny, so when you encounter certain trials, you are not taken by surprise. Just the opposite will be true in that you will have a plan of action already in place to adequately deal with the situation. It's better to make a misstep during the practice phase than when involved with clients, which could be ruinous for your enterprise and brand.

Try different methods to see what works and what doesn't. "Try, try, try, and keep on trying is the rule that must be followed to become an expert in anything," W. Clement Stone, businessman, philanthropist, and author expressed. Without utilizing your newly gained knowledge, you will not be prepared to overcome challenges and obstacles you are sure to encounter in the game of life. The trophy doesn't always go to the most talented. Yes, talent plays a large part, but it almost always comes down to what talents and gifts you have developed and continue to improve. Actor Will Smith has been called "the most powerful actor in Hollywood." Speaking on the art of practice, he said, "I've always considered myself to be just average talent and what I have is a ridiculous insane obsessiveness for practice and preparation."

I want to encourage you to be entirely prepared to step into your full destiny. Your expert knowledge and honed skills will make you stand out. You have already been gifted with talent, but that is not enough. To rise above the crowd and be regarded as a wise voice in your industry, make sure you practice. Strive for perfection in whatever you do, and practice is the best way to achieve excellence.

Make Mistakes

You read that correctly. Expect a bit of trial and error along the way, for it is almost guaranteed with any endeavor. I am not aware of any person who has reached the epitome of success to be immune from falls along the way. This is nothing to stress about, because you actually learn more from mistakes than from accolades. While it's inspiring to follow someone who is successful, the real lessons are in their mistakes and how they overcame their challenges. Those who are accomplished are often asked how they became successful, but rarely are they questioned about their oversights and faults. Hearing about someone's success does, in fact, encourage you, but what do we truly learn in hearing only the good? Although I am an advocate of speaking in the positive and remaining upbeat, there are times we need to hear the dirty and ugly of one's journey. Though they are victors now, what was it like for them to go through the difficulties and challenges that brought them to the present? What was that decision that took them to their lowest point financially, spiritually, and emotionally? What is that one thing they wish someone would have told them to keep them from making a mistake? Don't be intimidated not to ask these types of questions, for the insight gained from the answers contribute to developing competence. You will find that most successful people are more open to talking about their missteps, than their triumphs. When *Academy Award* winner Jane Fonda was asked about her career, she expressed, "You don't learn from successes; you don't learn from awards; you don't learn from celebrity; you only learn from wounds and scars and mistakes and failures. And that's the truth." Those who are accomplished have made mistakes and will continue to, for they are human. With wisdom and experience, they make fewer mistakes. You, too, will have mishaps, but know that victory will be waiting for you at the finish line. When you fall, get right back up.

In my encounters speaking worldwide on this topic, it has become very clear that our experiences and what we learn from them are not just for us, but for those who come after us. Equally so, mistakes are meant to be shared. They are nothing to be ashamed of or to hide from. People respect you for sharing your struggles, as well as that you didn't let them keep you down. Just as others share their experiences with you, share yours with the next generation and those who want to follow in your footsteps. Don't think of mistakes as a negative. I know that is not common thinking, but we are independent thinkers, right? Shift your mind-set and look at errors more as exploits. Adventures are exciting, and you should consider this period of your life as such. Your "adventures" will make you stronger and through that strength, you will gain unlimited possibilities. Success comes from snafus.

Use Your Gifts and Knowledge

"True happiness involves the full use of one's power and talents," said John William Gardner, Secretary of Health, Education, and Welfare under President Lyndon Johnson.

You have studied your industry and competitors, you have practiced, but now it's time to use your gifts and knowledge in real-life situations to create success. At this point, you are moving into your territory as an expert. The work starts here, and you are more than prepared for it. Your confidence in your authority of your business should be at its highest level. Trepidation is not in your vocabulary because your practice phase, or boot camp, has made you ready.

Unfortunately, many people don't use their gifts, because they have allowed fear to hold them back from living a higher life. This is a sad truth for countless individuals. People who do not use their gifts risk losing them. And this applies to knowledge and understanding. For example, let me take you back to your school days. After you studied a section of a textbook and practiced using the material, you took the exam, during which you were questioned about the material you learned. But, what if you were to take an Algebra test today? My guess is that you have lost your knowledge, because you've not used it for many years. Don't forfeit your gifts and skills, because of lack of use. In your calling, don't just pass the "exam." Ace it through all of your preparation and practice, which makes you proficient in your purpose.

Operating in your purpose means you will not let even one day go by without using your skills and knowledge. Your destiny will automatically attract opportunities to you. Even when you are not thinking about it, unlimited possibilities will fall into your lap. Being an authority, others will regard you highly. In turn, their esteem will cause more people to seek you out, resulting in opportunities beyond what you can imagine. Once you start to use what you have learned, you will unlock the door to a whole new sphere.

Use your gifts, talents, and abilities. How diligent you are in using them will determine how far you go in your future. Be confident and remember that if you don't use it, you will lose it.

Be Dedicated to Your Future

How dedicated are you to your future? When you perform work out of devotion, your heart is invested in the task. Experts are wholly devoted to their fields and the people they serve. For them, what they do is not just a job or a career, but a destiny and calling. When you are dedicated to your purpose, you handle it with loyalty and integrity.

You have formed a relationship between you and your gifts. Just like a friendship, you have to respect this relationship and be dedicated to it to see it grow. Of course, you need a break from work to rest your mind and clear your head to reboot. This is normal and healthy. What is not acceptable is when the break outweighs your action. Victors remain dedicated to their gifts. They understand that to be an expert, they must remain committed to the calling.

When I speak of commitment, I am not only referring to time. You will also have to invest energy and money. In the beginning phases on your journey to living in your calling, capital might be scarce. You might not have many clients or any investors, but with hard work and a wise strategy, over time, you definitely will have funds. However, humble beginnings are all part of the journey, as they keep you respectful and grateful. So, remember that investing in oneself includes time, effort, and finances.

Research rags-to-riches or success stories of today's great business leaders you hold in high regard. We see champions all polished, put together, and prosperous now. But, don't forget that they had to start at the bottom. With media and other sources painting unrealistic pictures of what it takes to be successful, too many people want what they want *now*. These influences, though entertaining, can make one believe that success comes easy. A "microwave success" mind-set is a major problem. It is not reality. Be patient and dedicated to the process.

Being called to this leadership purpose, you have a great responsibility to be devoted. It is not just so you can be successful, but because others will follow your example. Carlos Ghosn, Chairman of the Board of Nissan Motor Company said this about dedication: "Any job very well done that has been carried out by a person who is fully dedicated is always a source of inspiration." You were not given your special purpose just for you, but for others. People are watching you, so be dedicated. Be an inspiration.

Don't Abuse Your Gifts

When you are basking in the sunlight of success, your self-confidence is at its highest peak. You should feel a great sense of accomplishment and joy living in your purpose-filled life. But don't let your heightened self-esteem turn into a conceited spirit, for this will turn into pride. Nothing is wrong with success, but without even realizing it, you can abuse your gifts when egotism grips your heart. When you rise to the top in your field, your status and notoriety rises, as well. People start to seek your guidance and expert opinion. You become highly regarded in your field for your works and accomplishments. You should be celebrated. Who doesn't like a little spotlight? But don't let all the shine blind you to the fact that you are not God. Do not develop an overly high opinion of how important you are or *think* you are.

Abusing your gifts often makes you unaware of certain bad behaviors. For example, you could act as though you are more important than others around you, even those who helped you to flourish in your gift, such as employees or clients. Also, your newfound importance may have you making decisions that are best for you, but not necessarily for others involved in your business. Too many bad decisions could leave you in the red, with few opportunities, and a disgruntled team who feels unvalued.

True leaders are humble. They don't need to be seen, though their gifts put them on a public platform. Be humble always, remembering that your gifts were especially designed for and given to you. Anything given can be taken away. Any abuse of your gifts can cause an unfulfilled destiny, leaving you, as well as your purpose, unfulfilled.

When you are an authority in your field, your title doesn't change who you are. Use your gifts to change the world for the better. Your effective leadership doesn't allow you to abuse your gifts but instead, produces a heart to create change for the greater good and the betterment of others. *True* experts understand that their gifts are bigger than themselves, and they are selfless in their destiny.

As a high achiever, you have a raised awareness about your gifts, and you have a deeper understanding of the responsibility and respect for them. Even if you are not fully living in your purpose now, or if you are working for someone else, be an expert in whatever position you hold. That's right! You may not be a top executive yet, but work your position as if you are already where you aspire to be. Stay grateful, while going for greater. You will encounter learning experiences in every phase of your life, and you can miss them if you're complaining in the present. Your positive mind-set will keep your spirits high, continuing to sustain you, as you move forward on your path to reaching your goals and living in your desired destiny.

Now, don't think I can write on this topic without having learned these lessons from my own experiences. My words come sincerely and

UNLIMITED POSSIBILITIES

honestly from my heart and soul. There was a time when I was not an authority in my field, and I suffered consequences, as a result. Not being an expert not only affected my life, but also those around me. I could do better, yet I didn't. I could give more, but I didn't. That type of thinking was nothing but pure laziness. I was remiss when I did not become more knowledgeable in my purpose. Please learn from my mistakes.

One of the biggest lessons I learned from not being an expert was the impact on my income. Your yield will always be limited by how much you know. When you are an expert, you increase your earnings. Remember my words regarding the link between being an expert and your bottom line: "Learn more and earn more!" It may be simple, but it is so true. In my previous work experience, I thought that the people who were working in my same field were making more than I was, because they were so much better. I worked hard, spent countless hours on a project, but still saw no increase in my pay and had no real security within the company. Those who were authorities had higher value, helping the company run more efficiently. When layoffs occurred, those with greater knowledge and well-honed skills didn't get a pink slip. Finally, I had my light-bulb moment that kicked me in the pants and gave me a reality check. I saw that my counterparts stood apart from me, because they had greater knowledge than I did. People in my industry were making ten times, even one-hundred times, more than me, and they were valued more, because they had studied and gained special knowledge in their field. I was working harder, but not smarter. Part of working smarter is becoming an expert.

When you are an authority, you are intentional about your purpose. Not being intentional results in a very poor strategy. My strategy needed to change. I needed to be an expert in my field. We need to stop telling people to just be *good enough*. While I was *good enough* at completing my assignments, that wasn't enough to unlock unlimited possibilities. Settling for *good enough* means you don't want a better life bad enough. I was comfortable and complacent. I understand why many are ashamed to admit that. I was there, but once I spoke it aloud, I could not blame the supervisor, my colleagues, or the industry. I was where I was in life, because of where I chose to be. If you are complacent where you are, it's time to get out of your comfort zone and start taking risks that will produce rewards. Boxing great Muhammad Ali was known for getting people out of their comfort zones with his celebrated style in the ring and with his words. "He who is not courageous enough to take risks will accomplish nothing in life" is one of the greatest quotes regarding getting out of one's comfort zone. Our decisions and strategies can keep us to be *good enough* or to be *greater*. I had to change my strategy.

Another thing I realized was that I had set the bar for myself way too low. When I went into entrepreneurship, I raised the standard for myself. If I wanted to earn more, give more to my industry, and serve my clientele with the highest standard, I had to increase my knowledge specific to my field. I couldn't just scratch the surface of research. I had to dig deep to become an expert.

Possessing this level of understanding, you will want your team to increase their knowledge, also. You cannot know everything. Trying to do it all will spread yourself thin. Great leaders separate themselves from lesser leaders when they aren't afraid to bring in effective personnel with exceptional skills who are more gifted in an area than they are. Admit that you don't know everything, that you are not always the smartest person in the room. True leadership is neither egotistical nor intimidated by the intelligent.

One of the greatest benefits to being an authority is being peaceful and calm. My sense of awareness has been elevated, and the things I once fixated on no longer concern me. Even though business is about profits, I don't view money as I did before I started living in my destiny. The money is great, and it almost always comes with increased responsibility, but my income is not my foundation for living in my destiny. My focus is doing what I was put on this earth for. My success is the freedom to do what I love to do, while making a positive impact on people's lives through my work. I am fulfilled. When you are living a life with intention and purpose, you walk different, talk different, live different, and even breathe different. This is true success.

Doors will open for you when you distinguish yourself. Unleash the unlimited possibilities through your decision-making processes. When you rise above the crowd, unlimited possibilities are unlocked. It is amazing. I have received invitations to sit with presidents and kings, because of my expert knowledge. When you are an authority in your field, you join a network of others who share this level of expertise.

The expert is within you, so let me encourage you to do whatever it requires to tap into your *inner expert*. Gaining knowledge and developing your gifts make the difference between being just good at what you do and being *exceptional*. Respect the process. Respect your gifts. Be an expert.

QUESTIONS

1. What obstacles have been keeping you from obtaining greater knowledge in your field?

2. How can you overcome these obstacles?

3. Name two or three great leaders you admire. How will you apply their practices to your life, so you can create success?

4. What methods will you use, so you can become an authority and "learn more and earn more"?

5. When you become an expert, in what ways will it benefit your life?

6. If you choose not to be an expert, how will your life be?

CHAPTER 7
POWER IN FAILURE

The "F" Word

Men learn little from success, but much from failure.

~Arabian Proverb

CHAPTER 7
POWER IN FAILURE

The "F" Word

Great power is in failure. This is not considered the *normal* way of thinking, but how far has conventional thinking gotten you in your quest for success? Please realize that there is absolutely nothing normal about the way independent thinkers think.

Concerning failure and accomplishments, standard is not in our jargon. Great leaders, who are independent thinkers, are able to tap into the power that is deep within, in order to succeed, despite the bleakest of situations. Some of the most powerful leaders in the world were once considered failures. But, for every person who sees failure as a negative, I can show you a hundred millionaires, once deemed defeated, who will tell you the exact opposite—that failure is enlightening. Exceptional leaders are not unrealistic about opposition. But, they see beyond the present situation to a more profitable future. Leaders with an unparalleled level of thinking do not consider where they will be if they don't give up; rather, they think about what they will never become if they quit. When society tells you not to surround yourself with failures, I tell you to find some "failures," and then transition from good enough to superior leadership. Whether your purpose has called you to be a CEO, a business executive, an entrepreneur, an executive director of a non-profit, or any other leadership role, find yourself some failures and gain insight and wisdom from them.

Thomas Edison, businessman and American inventor asserted, "I have not failed ten thousand times. I have not failed once. I have succeeded in proving that those ten thousand ways will not work. When I have eliminated the ways that will not work, I will find the way that will work." Many people thought of Edison as a failure. Teachers labeled him "too stupid to learn anything." He was fired from his first two jobs for being "nonproductive." If Edison had listened to these people and conceded, he would not be renowned and esteemed as America's greatest inventor.

Because of Edison's determination, his story continues to encourage countless others to keep working toward their goals. Think about it this way. If Edison had deserted his destiny, how many of his one-thousand-plus inventions would the world be without? His inventions have so impacted our society that he continues to be regarded as the greatest inventor of all time.

But, greatness doesn't come without its share of challenges. Before the accolades is the story. No one who has risen to significance does so without a testimony. Edison had a story, because he pushed through when his challenges tried to deter him, when his teachers dubbed him addled, and wrote him off as a failure. But, rather than listen to the naysayers in his life, he listened to his heart.

You are in the midst of your story, and if you want it to be told, you can't quit because someone says you can't accomplish what you dream of. Remember that your story is never just for you, but for those who come after you. People will walk in your path and will face your same challenges. They will be encouraged to persevere, because you did. Don't give in. Your story needs to be told.

No matter how many times you fall, don't give in to the inclination to quit. That feeling to give in is fear, a trick of the enemy playing with your subconscious to make you think that the current setback is permanent. Don't let your emotions get the best of you. Fight the feeling that you will not recover from the present obstacle and persevere toward your purpose.

Are you dealing with disappointment or failure right now? Let me assure you that this is part of the journey that will contribute to your personal development. This is the time to find the power in your failure that will change your outlook and approach; thereby, stimulating your success and moving you forward.

When dealing with failure, you must shift your focus, forgetting everything you were ever taught about failure. Alter your thought patterns for a fresh perspective on failure regarding business or any area in your life. Start thinking like Edison and view failure as learning how *not* to do something. It may feel peculiar, as it's not the customary way of thinking. But, the distinction between mediocrity and immeasurable achievement is the mental process. Notable leaders push through, not really seeing the failure as an obstacle, as their peers do, but as an opportunity. And an opportunity, usually a very lucrative one, is exactly what they make out of their failures. As the old saying goes, "If life gives you lemons, make lemonade." Whatever your "lemons," know that you can turn them into sweet and stellar success.

Let's breakdown F-A-I-L-U-R-E:

F: Failure Is FEEDBACK

Fail early, fail often, and learn from your failures in this game of life. Failure is invaluable feedback. Bill Gates spoke on failure: "It's fine to celebrate success, but it is more important to heed the lessons of failure." Mistakes are memorable. The next time you encounter that same situation, stop and think before you act; recalling the result of that past failure and considering what adjustments you should make. There is a high probability that you will not commit the same mistake again and instead, produce a different and more favorable outcome. When you are suffering deep disappointment, your spirit is low and you feel regret. I know that it seems hard to do in the moment, but don't look at the failure with sorrow and regret. Instead, look at the failure as feedback. What is the message in your current "failure"? The setback is speaking to you, but if you allow room for self-pity, it will be hard for you to hear that voice.

As a great leader, it's not wrong to have negative feelings after a misfortune. However, don't wallow in them. Find the feedback in your failure, renew your purpose, and move forward. Learning experiences are found in the failure. Learn from them, lean on them, but don't live in them.

A: Failure Makes You APPRECIATIVE

If failure makes you appreciative are you supposed to say, "Thank you, failure?" No, not at all. No accomplished person enjoys encountering failure or defeat, but in these failures are lessons we could learn no other way. Be thankful for what you have taken away from the experience.

Some things can be learned only in hardship. The teaching is in the setbacks and overcoming, which must happen before true success can emerge. Failure opens your eyes, giving you a radical sense of awareness about yourself. Failure lets you chew on a little humble pie, adjusting your attitude, which results in a transformation that allows you to lead differently and more effectively.

Appreciate that the failure occurred early in your process, rather than further along. Appreciate that the failure cost you less of your profits than it could have. Appreciate that you have overcome, and that you are stronger and sharper than before. Also, be thankful for what did not occur. "It could be worse," is a familiar cliché, but it is absolute truth. I'm not asking you to be joyous and content in the failure, but being appreciative for the failure, and what you learn from it is necessary for you to move forward toward your destiny. Your attitude of appreciation will unleash unlimited possibilities.

I: Failure Makes You INGENIOUS

Think back to a time when you were in a *do-or-die* situation. What was your mind-set? Did you want to give up? Did you look around for someone to get you out of your state? Or, did you determine to find a way out?

Ingenuity requires discernment. Being ingenious calls for resourcefulness and thinking creatively. This is how strong leaders handle crises. They are pioneers who apply strategic desperation to their apparent failures.

Don't look at *desperation* as a bad expression. Being desperate in certain situations is unhealthy and can cause unfavorable results. However, for your purpose, positive desperation is the attitude of tapping into your resources. Your directed desperation provides perseverance to make a way out of what most people believe there's no way out. When the situation is dire, your strategic desperation births in you a determination to turn the failure into something positive.

Being committed to your purpose means having no choice but to work/think through the seeming failure. Times like these are when you rise to the occasion and exceed not only others' expectations of you, but also your own. How bad do you want what you're working toward? When times are tough, you will answer that question through your ability to continue to move toward your goals.

Your desire to advance in your career, build your business, or achieve your personal goals may force you to be more imaginative in your quest for success. When great leaders are faced with losing everything, it drives them to be inventive. They push through with excellence and think through every result before creating and implementing a plan of action. Let failures compel you to think outside of the box to gain effective and positive results.

When faced with opposition, great or small, use your ingenuity. Your true management skills will shine through.

L: Failure Makes You a Strong LEADER

Failure will put you through the fire, but it will definitely take you higher, making you a more influential leader. Failure allows you to see not only what didn't work, but also what did or could work, giving you a new plan that will move your destiny forward. I stress the benefit of mistakes and challenges, because learning what not to do is invaluable in your purpose. Having experienced what not to do is like a child burning his hand on a hot iron or hot stove. He takes away from that experience that he must make different choices to avoid being hurt or experiencing pain and other consequences. What not to do may become your lifeline.

Your leadership skills are sharpened after a failure, making you stronger, wiser, and more confident in your capabilities. The disappointments bring out your undiscovered abilities, allowing you to tap into your inner strength. When your attitude is right, despite the circumstances, your faith and patience are made stronger. Failure makes you aware of qualities within yourself that you didn't know existed. Simply put, it is like digging for undiscovered gold. Obstacles can drive you to search out your "gold," characteristics and talents you otherwise would not identify had you never faced difficulties. Difficult times bring out the best in you, building you into the leader you were destined to be.

U: Failure Makes You UNAFRAID.

The business branding geniuses behind the *No Fear* apparel line sum up my sentiments perfectly regarding leadership: no fear! It seems simple, but straightforward is sometimes enlightening. Having no fear in tight situations seems easier said than done, but the important thing to remember is that it can be done. These two words will take you farther than you can image if you continue to push forward and follow the path toward your purpose.

Of course, you may experience some anxiety and concern when facing failure. These are common human emotions. If I told you I have never felt anxiety, I would be deceiving you. But as a leader, you cannot be afraid to tackle any task that is demanded of you. The battle is in your mind regarding what you can and cannot do. Think on a higher level, more spiritual, if you will.

I am a firm believer in faith and that your spiritual life is the foundation for your "un-fear." It is not that you won't have moments of apprehension. But, with the hope and conviction you possess, know that despite how difficult the stumbling block is in front of you, a great reward is on the other side of it.

Let me offer another perspective. Could the reward of conflicts and obstacles be the responsibility of solving and overcoming these challenges themselves? Read that sentence again and think on it. Out of all the individuals on the planet, the universe purposed you in this place and time. This responsibility to prepare you for your purpose is meant just for you. You have been chosen for a reason. You have no need to be afraid.

R: Failure Makes You RESILIENT

After conquering a failure, you feel like a superhero. Seriously! You have climbed the mountain and are now at the top. You conquered the obstacle, as well as fear, and overcame both. Now, you can breathe!

Workout enthusiasts experience a surge of endorphins—the feel-good hormone—after a tough and rigorous workout. Corporate professionals feel a similar surge after pulling an all-nighter to meet an important deadline. I have felt that many times. It is the sensation or success. Fighting through a difficulty gives such a rush of adrenaline that you may feel invincible and maybe even unbreakable.

Resiliency makes you remarkable, giving you the capacity to recover quickly from struggles. Defeating major challenges, not giving up, toughens you. It's not arrogance or self-importance; rather, it's the feeling of accomplishment.

I am sure we agree that we do not wish difficulty into our lives. However, if you've overcome difficulties, and grown stronger and wiser as a result, you can be confident that you will be able to withstand and recover quickly from future challenges and continue moving toward your destiny. Remember, all challenges are nothing but new opportunities for you to *strut your stuff* as a champion. Stand tall! You wear an "S" on your chest.

E: Failure Brings You ELEVATION

I have saved the absolute best for last! You are without a doubt elevated after a failure. By "elevated," I mean that you are now poised for greater opportunities. Your confidence and self-worth have increased. Your abilities have heightened. You are prepared to make better business and career decisions. The problems of the past have prepared you for prosperity.

The hardship, difficulty, and challenge you went through have changed how you approach your purpose, business, or project. That failure will not prevent or hinder your progress, unless you allow it to. Having conquered the obstacle, your mind-set is on the amazing journey ahead of you, not what is behind you. You bring the lessons with you, but the past hurt and pain remain behind. Because you process "failure" differently now, you do not want any excess baggage to impede your elevation. You have room for only unlimited possibilities.

Your attitude of gratitude is also greater. You are more appreciative for the *Law of Preparation* and understand its importance. It is like a total life-altering transformation. You can accomplish anything you put your mind to.

Looking at failure with this new perspective can transform you from a *ho-hum* leader into a superlative leader. You are in new territory. Embrace it. Revel in it. No longer will you just survive. Now, you will thrive.

Lessons to Learn from Failure

Failure is not a bad word. As I said before, where most people consider failure as a negative, we victors have fixed our minds on the positive. We are not unrealistic, but our outlook is on opportunities, instead of opposition. Your mind-set matters, for therein lies the battle. With a firm belief in the power of a positive attitude, Winston Churchill said, "Attitude is a little thing that makes a big difference." Pastor, author, and educator Charles R. Swindoll said, "Attitude is more important than the past, than education, than money, than circumstances, than what people do or say. It is more important than appearance, giftedness, or skill."

To make it through tough or even dark times, your attitude will make the difference between being broken by the situation or overcoming it. Have you ever wondered how someone went from homeless to Harvard? Did you ever consider what brought someone with nothing to someone with much? The transition into their unlimited possibilities was all because of how they set their thoughts. The attitude itself does not solve the complication. Neither does it produce a quick fix. But, what it does give is the clear-cut ability to focus on solutions over problems.

As a great leader, your determination to move into your destiny, despite difficulties, positions you to receive endless opportunities. To succeed, tap into the power that is already inside of you. When situations seem grave your attitude, which is set on overcoming obstacles, lets you see a breakthrough.

Burdens teach us something about failure and about ourselves, as we touched on earlier. My success as a business coach is not only a result of hard work and faith, but also my personal experiences with failure. These enable me to offer solid, workable advice to my clients and those I speak to. We all have a personal story about failure. A motivational speaker can encourage you with his or her story of failure, but your first-hand knowledge with difficulty gives true revelation.

I did not grow up in a wealthy family. In fact, I grew up in poverty. You may have heard the term *dirt poor*. I lived it. In my young adulthood, while searching for a better life in Finland, I ended up homeless. Ironic, isn't it? But, that was one of many invaluable experiences in which I learned the truth and lessons about failure. Going to Finland, I knew no one and had less than five-hundred euro's—about $600 USD. Young and naïve, I soon found myself dead broke and destitute.

Lesson One

You find yourself in situations that are disastrous, because you fail to plan and have unrealistic expectations. While it is great to step out in faith to live your dreams, make sure you have prepared a way to support yourself, while pursuing them.

With no finances or permanent work, I was forced to clean the restrooms of the local pubs or wherever anyone would hire me. To make additional income, I sold soft drink bottles that I collected from dumpsters and garbage cans in parks, movie theaters, and elsewhere just so I could have money for sustenance. My meager budget allowed meals of noodles—only noodles.

Lesson Two

Failure will force you to be resourceful and humble. How are you going to make a way out of no way? Failure pushes your mind to think creatively to meet your needs and wants. You cannot be too good to do anything when you are desperate. Pride goes out the door when you are facing failure. Don't starve on the road to success, because of misplaced pride.

Being homeless and living on the streets and in shelters, I felt so alone. Let me tell you something about being homeless. You are looked down upon as if you are nothing and that you don't matter. People judge you, assuming you are a vagrant, because you are a criminal or an addict. You are ignored. I can recall countless times when people looked down when I passed them, not wanting to make eye contact with me. I felt as if I didn't exist. Even though I was praying to God, I must admit that my faith was tested.

Lesson Three

Failure forces you to be compassionate toward others and to view human beings without preconceived notions. Being judged and stereotyped when you are at your lowest teaches you to see others as individuals, not as a group or as a stereotype. You won't make the mistake of assuming the worst as to why they are in their particular situation.

Thankfully, I met someone who had mercy on me. In exchange for helping provide food, meager as it was, he gave me a place sleep on the floor of his one-bedroom apartment. That may not seem like much, but having been homeless for so long, it seemed like winning the lottery.

Sleeping on the streets and in facilities for the homeless is not safe. I was thankful for a secure place to rest my head and to bathe. A month later, I received my first permanent job, performing cleaning duties at a restaurant. I learned that faith and attitude can attract acts of genuine kindness from strangers.

Lesson Four

Failure forces you to remain faithful, which releases God's grace and mercy that He provides through His angels on earth. Faith is sometimes all you have during a failure, so don't lose it. Faith can allow God to work in ways you cannot imagine. Good people are in the world, so always remember that human decency still exists.

Lesson Five

You are more inclined to pay it forward when you are faced with failure. Pay forward the kindness given to you.

Reflecting on Failure

My homelessness was just one of many times I encountered extreme challenges. However, I could not let that defeat me. Life-changing lessons come from those hardships. Had I not experienced being homeless, I would have missed those valuable truths that eventually equipped me with what I needed to move forward into several successful endeavors.

When you encounter failure, reflection is key to future achievements. Focus on past successes. Look back to a time when you were up against the wall and it seemed like that deal wouldn't go through. Then, at the last moment, everything fell into place and you sealed the deal. Remember when you were working out of your studio apartment and could barely make ends meet? Well, look at you now, great leader! Remember where you started from and compare that with where you are now. You deserve a big pat on the back! If you created something great with very few assets, imagine how much more you can accomplish now that you have more. This time around, you have more experience, contacts, resources, and you are more motivated than ever. Always reflect on the positives, shifting your focus to success.

Unless you want to stay in perpetual failure, make no room in your life for a negative mind-set. Always be looking toward advancing your business. As a business owner or CEO, you have to be selfless, being constantly aware that you are not just succeeding for yourself. Team members, employees, and your support system, as well as your clients and customers, are depending on you.

As the person at the top, it starts with you. Your attitude, positive or negative, is infectious. It flows from you to your team and others involved in fulfilling your destiny. It may be uncomfortable while you are in the midst of the consequences of your current failure, but growth is also a by-product of failure. Remember to keep that positive perspective. Some of my biggest failures came after I achieved success. However, I didn't let the failures keep me down. I reflected on what didn't work, thought through some other options, and then got busy putting my plan into action. Just like I conquered my challenges, and continue to do so, you can too.

You read earlier about the *Discovery Zone*. When things don't work out in life as you planned, you are tempted to call yourself a failure. That is flat-out not true! It's possible that your plan wasn't the best choice for you. That's where the *Discovery Zone* can help.

Let's say you've chosen to pursue a career as a building contractor. You decided upon this because you come from a family of contractors, you've been building since you were a young teenager, and you already have an established network of suppliers and subcontractors. This choice makes sense. But, if you base your career choice solely on what "makes sense" without considering the small voice within you that's calling you toward your passion and purpose, you could be setting yourself up for failure. You may have all the skills to be a great builder, but what is that worth if you are not fulfilled or content? This lack of deep satisfaction that comes from ignoring your inner voice is a tragic kind of failure.

You can bring failure into your life when you don't listen to your inner spirit guiding you. At first, you may not "hear" that gentle voice, but you sense deep within you a calling to something. Be patient, as you listen to it.

You have probably heard people say that you can be whatever you want if you just believe and put your heart into it. That encouragement typically comes from a sincere heart, but it is just not true. For example, a fish can put its heart and mind into working toward the goal of thriving on land. It will never succeed. It is designed and destined to live and thrive in water. Is it a failure if it cannot live on land? No. The fish is not a failure. The process failed, because land was not where the fish was ever meant to be.

Things don't work out as planned or you don't thrive in certain settings, because that is not your purpose. We will never be fully successful, or even partially successful, when we work against what we were born for.

If you feel like a failure right now, it could be because you are not where you were designed to be. When you try to force the purpose you want, or others want for you, you are inviting into your life unnecessary challenges.

Failure can occur in your life when:

- you do not know who you are;

- you have not tapped into your God-given abilities and strengths;

- you are doing what brings others (e.g., family members) fulfillment in their lives;

- you have not completed the *Discovery Zone* process with an open heart and mind.

Honestly, consider the above points. Do any describe you? Are you failing to live in your genuine purpose? Revisit the *Discovery Zone*, if necessary. Following *your* destiny doesn't guarantee a perfect life, but it promises greater fulfillment and satisfaction, and you will avoid many unnecessary complications.

People who were labeled (by teachers, family members, friends, etc.) as failures are some of the most successful today. Breaking down failure with my method may be unconventional, but it has been my tried-and-true template for triumph. I think like Edison. See the opposite of what others see regarding failure. Failure is not a bad word; rather, it is a springboard for greater things. There is great power in failure.

QUESTIONS

1. Have you completed the *Discovery Zone?*

2. How do you currently view failure?

3. Looking at a past or recent failure, give one element for each word, as we broke down F-A-I-L-U-R-E in this chapter.

4. Thomas Edison endured naysayers in his life. Have you experienced those types of individuals? What steps can you take to refuse to let their words impact your purpose?

5. Who is one successful person you admire in your field? Research that person's failure(s). If you have a relationship with him or her, conduct an interview. What did he or she do to overcome a failure? How did that inspire you to move forward when faced with obstacles?

6. Do you view failure differently now? In what way(s)?

7. What is your new definition of failure?

CHAPTER 8
TAKEOFF

Time to Fly!

Actions are the seed of fate; deeds grow into destiny.

~Harry S. Truman

CHAPTER 8
TAKEOFF

Time to Fly!

Picture this: It's early Monday morning, and you have arrived at the airport. After going through security, you do a quick scan to find a place to grab a cup of strong coffee. It's going to be a long, but productive day. Once you arrive at your gate, you take a seat and check out the latest news headlines on your mobile device and slowly sip on your satisfying stimulant, enjoying the peace and quiet of the early morning. As time passes, the Monday morning business commuters fill the airport halls with their scurrying. It's time to board, and they call your section. You take your seat on the plane, buckle up, get comfortable, and wait for takeoff. After the captain makes his announcements, the plane speeds down the runway. You have flown several times before, but the butterflies always seem to flutter in your stomach before takeoff. Wheels up and the plane elevates higher toward the clouds. You feel peace, as you take in the wonders of the blue sky. What was anticipation is now a state of calmness.

My friends, you are ready to depart for your destiny. You are at your gate of greatness, and it is time to take off into your unlimited possibilities. No more are you a drifter and wanderer. You have created your launching pad that will send you to your destiny to fulfill your purpose. Whatever your dreams and goals are now is the time to take off. You cannot stay in the present and expect to reap success. Move forward where you reward is waiting. It is up to you to take that first step. That business, that nonprofit, that promotion, that financial freedom ... they are all yours for the taking. This is your time to become airborne.

The airplane analogy seems fitting. But, there's another reason I chose it. I am a pilot. Are you surprised? You shouldn't be. Earlier, I referred to Pastor T.D. Jakes as he reminded us that there is not a period behind our names, but a comma. I live by that each and every day, living life to the fullest. I am an international business coach, entrepreneur, and philanthropist, but my passion for flying is just as strong as my enthusiasm for business and giving.

Let me remind you of the importance of surrounding yourself with like-minded people. Those in your circle should encourage you to do more, no matter what level you are already achieving at. A friend encouraged and challenged me to receive my pilot's license. He is typical of those in my circle. They do not put themselves into a box, and neither do I. You should not do that, either. No law says that you have to stay in a certain place all your life. You are about to take off to your destiny. You have no limit as to who you are or how far you can go. You have no need to stop short of your potential. No period is behind your name. You don't write a last chapter for your life, because your options are unnumbered.

You must believe you can do it, even when the circumstances seem to say you *cannot*. Again, I stress the importance of your faith on this journey. Serial entrepreneur and author Erica Dias authored *Faith It, Until You Make It*. What keeps her and other successful movers and shakers traveling on the journey of championship? It is pure and unbreakable faith. With faith is a strong belief that things are possible, even when they seem impossible. Hold on to faith, believing the imaginable when the situation seems unimaginable. I used the word *seems* for a reason. It doesn't matter how things appear. What does matter is that you keep your focus on the unlimited possibilities. More often than not, they are hiding in "cannot" circumstances.

But, in order to walk through open doors of opportunities, you have to first believe that they are available to you. I continue to unleash my unlimited possibilities with a *can-do* mind-set. These two little words are more than just an expression; they create bliss and blessings in your purpose. You can do absolutely anything you desire.

UNLIMITED POSSIBILITIES

You've probably heard the term *can do* many times. Let's break down this favored expression. *Can* is a verb, meaning that you have the ability to do something. Also a verb, *do* means to perform. As independent thinkers who operate at higher levels, this little phrase tells us that we have the ability to perform whatever we put our minds to. If you desire—a prerequisite for unlimited possibilities—to unleash a better life, then you must take action. Accompanying your positive psyche and belief are the appropriate action steps.

One of my methods to create a positive mind-set is an acronym of characteristics for *can do*. "Can do" people are described as follows:

Certain

People who are ready to take off are certain about who they are and where they are going. They are set to soar into their rightful place of success. You must be certain of yourself as an individual, understand what your gifts are, and clearly know your destiny and purpose before you can take off. These together provide your flight plan with specific details for your particular destiny. If you don't know where you are going, then you cannot be certain of your goals and your precise place in this universe.

Doubt and confusion cannot release you into your destiny, for where would you go? This is why you must complete your *Discovery Zone* (see chapter two). Would it surprise you to learn that many champions had to tackle the *Discovery Zone* more than once? I am one of them. In life, certain opportunities can make you believe that a specific thing is your purpose, but as you go farther along, you come to realize that those opportunities were not, in fact, leading you to your destiny. You should feel no shame in repeating this process. Always remember that it is better to do the *Discovery Zone* again, than to be doubtful and unclear, questioning your destiny. Being certain does not mean that you will know every single detail for your life. Some things God must keep a mystery for the strengthening of our faith. No one knows their exact future and every single circumstance they will encounter in life. But with certainty, one has complete confidence that they are traveling in the right direction. With assurance, faith, and focus, victorious territory is just beyond the horizon.

Able

Before you take off, you must be absolutely able. Taking off requires you to be more than just considerably skilled, intelligent, and proficient. Those who are successful have created favorable circumstances through their actions. Something marvelous happens when you become able. Doors begin to open to your unlimited possibilities, as you take action in your one-of-a-kind abilities. Don't believe that some kind of magical powers are releasing you into universal promises. The "magic" is in your ability, as well as using your ability. You were provided talents and gifts, so that you can use them to their fullest. Great things don't happen with just the possession of purposeful powers. You must apply your ability to your dreams and goals to bring them into reality.

On the other hand, when things are not going smoothly, are you able to continue on the path? The takeoff doesn't always occur on a nicely paved runway. Sometimes, it's a bumpy dirt road. Your conviction turns the ignition for you to take off. Jürgen Norbert Klopp is a German football manager and former professional player who pronounced, "Anyone can have a good day, but you have to be able to perform on a bad day." You are easily able to execute your plan when the sky is blue, but when you hit a little turbulence, the persistence to push through can be a little problematic. Being able is not sufficient for you to achieve. But when you are able, you become tough enough to push through the pursuit on your purpose. Endless possibilities are hidden within the crevices of difficulties, sacrifices, and challenges. Just like you are able when the sun is shining, don't lose your ability when there is a little rain. For after the rain comes your reward of the rainbow.

Necessary

Achievers understand that knowing their purpose and destiny are necessary for success to be realized. While we enjoy the fruits of our labor and the perks that come with hard work and dedication, we must remember that our purpose is never for our own benefit. We each were chosen for special gifts before we were even born. And the wonderful thing is that no two gifts are the same. Even though we may share similar gifts, our capacity differs when serving a specific function.

UNLIMITED POSSIBILITIES

Many special ingredients go into an award-winning cake. If you use only flour or milk, you won't end up with a cake. But, when you also combine eggs, oil, sugar, and other special ingredients, you will end up with something delicious and satisfying! The world is extensive and the needs are great. If we all had an identical destiny certain needs would go unmet, even ignored. The more that gifts and talents are divided, the larger the impact for the greater good. In the same way, successful people do not take all of the credit for their companies' reaching monumental achievement. Rather, it took a group of people with specialized knowledge and unique giftedness to make it happen.

Taking off, you left your ego at the door, appreciating that no one person accomplishes greatness on their own. From the secretary to the accountant and to the sales representative, the combined talents working with your leadership skills result in success. No two assignments are the same and will not reach the same group of people, but that does not mean one endeavor is greater or lesser than another. When you know that your talents are necessary, your outlook is balanced and realistic. You don't have a spirit of jealousy or unimportance. You have no need to compare yourself with others, and you have no need to be selfish. Seeing your purpose as service, you know that you are necessary to fulfill your unique purpose. It is not about accolades or stages, but about taking off into a purposeful place.

Rather than focus solely on the bottom line or the number of people in your audience, concentrate on being necessary. Think about it this way. Someone, somewhere in the universe, is waiting on you to perform the greatness of your purpose. When you are living in your destiny with the right mind-set, you meet others' needs, while attracting financial blessings.

Never forget that what you possess within you matters on several levels. Not only is it important to live to your potential, but also your gifts and abilities are to help others excel in their lives. We are responsible for others.

Isn't it wonderful to know that you were thought of enough to be gifted with this level of leadership?

Deliberate

When you take off, you have put on a state of mind to function in your purpose! You should not be doing things just to do them. We hear people say all the time that they are busy, but that doesn't mean they are productive. Be deliberate with each action you undertake in your destiny. You must be intentional in everything you do. Every force in your fate should have a focus and be leading you farther toward reaching your goals and objectives in your purpose. Being deliberate in your destiny, you will experience growth and wisdom.

Delegation is key. You cannot do everything, and you should not be working in every department within your company or organization. You cannot successfully lead a company, handle the customer service department, and be the marketing manager. Though you may know the workings of each department, you will spread yourself too thin working in several different areas. You will miss something. You cannot operate with excellence functioning this way. Don't be good or average at many things. Instead, be a high achiever in your main responsibility, which will then result in a more favorable outcome in the long-term.

Just like you must be conscientious and deliberate in your position, so must those on your team. As they are focused on their assignments, you will create a domino effect that will take you to your unlimited possibilities.

When you take off toward your destiny, something happens inside of you. Some describe it as a rush of adrenaline, as they travel in their exciting and new domain. Others express it as an eagerness to get to the next level. I want that feeling of extreme excitement for you. I get excited as a business coach to celebrate in one's new endeavors. But, what can happen in takeoff is that the exhilaration of moving toward your potential, you can want to do everything at all once. That makes you busy. Time is an important element, and busy does not necessarily equal profits or help you possess your purpose. Time is to be valued, and you should not waste a minute. But, don't go so fast that you forget to be deliberate and focused. And make sure any "to-do lists" you made are deliberate, leading you to your limitless options. They should not create busyness that will detour you from your ultimate goal. (See chapter three, Success List.)

Original

Every person on earth is an original. Even if you are a twin, you have characteristics and talents unique to you. As an independent thinker, you are aware of who you are and are confident in how your specific and distinctive abilities will benefit the world. This provides self-assurance when taking off into your destiny and purpose.

As an original, you are excited about the plans for your life. You don't waste time trying to live another's existence. How dry and uneventful would this planet be if we all were exactly the same! That robotic world would be mundane. Your originality is what makes you special and what makes an impact. You must be okay with being an original. Be content if you are not invited to the "cool kids" table. You have to be thick-skinned, because inevitably, some people will question your process and methods that may be different from the norm.

As an independent thinker, you are nonconforming, and normal is not in your vocabulary. In fact, being original, you create a new normal. How many successful people have been questioned and doubted regarding their ideas and methods, yet didn't give in to the pressures of others' close-minded criticism? Those who criticize and doubt don't achieve higher levels of success. They cannot get out of their heads that something can be done in a different way. Companies and entities that don't go against the grain can stay at their present level, face severe hardships, or go out of business. As the times change, you must think outside of the box and use originality with your abilities and skills. Those who are originals see their being different not as a bad thing. In fact, it is an appealing and refreshing quality. They would not be in this world making history without the courage of someone with an original outlook who took a risk.

Blockbuster not purchasing Netflix is still one of the most talked about stories in the business world. Back in 2000, Reed Hastings, founder of Netflix, approached former Blockbuster CEO John Antioco and offered to sell Netflix for $50 million. At that time, Netflix was a

DVD mailing service that was losing money, which prompted Hastings's decision to sell. Antioco refused the opportunity. Now, Netflix is worth over $32 billion dollars and available in forty countries.[1] If Antioco had the vision to see what Netflix could be, in spite of its losing money, he would be living a very different life than he is now. With original thinking outside of the box, he could be basking in the success that Netflix is experiencing today, or maybe he could've taken it even higher. I guess we will never know.

Other companies that missed out on opportunities that could have made a difference in the business world:

- Verizon shunned Apple for the first model of the iPhone;
- Comcast withdrew its bid for Disney;
- Friendster refused Google's offer of a buyout;
- AOL merging with Time Warner instead of AT&T;
- Yahoo not capitalizing on its chance to buy both Facebook and Google.

One of the greatest characteristics of an original is being able to see beyond the present state of something, envisioning what it can be, and then taking it from gutter to goldmine. An original thinker has a certain level of intelligence and unshakable faith to turn situations around that result in prosperity and unlimited possibilities.

Anything Is Possible

How can I be a businessman, a pilot, and do all that I do? Easy. It's because I believe and shift my mind to a place where anything is possible. Your unlimited possibilities are unleashed when you release yourself from a harness of complacency. Why can't I be a pilot? If you want something, go for it. That may sound like a cliché, but it isn't. It is how you live your life.

UNLIMITED POSSIBILITIES

I shared with you that I grew up far from prosperity, but even though I was raised with meager means, my thoughts were not meager. I thought higher than the place I was in. You may not be where you want to be, but your drive, determination, and desire for a better destination should allow your mind to look toward your future. Don't let the present keep your thoughts in the present. Instead, focus and fight for the future you long for.

When I was young and looked up and saw airplanes high in the sky, I told myself that when I became an adult, I would have wings and fly. Unlimited possibilities in a limited situation truly release strong momentum and resolution. If you are at the bottom, you really have nowhere to go but up. Being in extreme poverty, the total opposite of where I am today, provided motivation to fight to get out of my situation. It was not easy, but I knew there was no limit to what I could achieve when I set my mind to it. I knew I had a purpose, so I pursued it. After I became a pilot, I remembered those instances as a child seeing airplanes. Back then, I was actually affirming my desire and didn't even realize it. Looking deeper, one can even say my thinking was elevated in every area of my life. So, I am not just flying in airplanes, but in my dreams, goals, and aspirations.

Are you ready to take off? Do you have a flight plan? The pilot doesn't flip a coin to decide where she is going. You should have the unwavering desire to take off, and that energy is magnetic. But, with a positive attitude, you should have a plan for your purpose. Forethought is key to your reaching the high levels in your destiny. Breaking it down further, your flight plan tells you not only where you are going, but how you will get there. It's that simple. It is nothing more complicated than that. Life is not complicated, so don't overthink your plan for a prosperous life.

A pilot's flight plan takes into consideration unsettled weather, allowing the pilot to fly the plane successfully, properly, and strategically to the intended destination. It's not negative thinking to allow for bad weather; rather, it is realistic thinking and planning. In the same way, when devising your life plan, consider that there will be challenges somewhere along the way. Not to allow for possible difficulties is being ill-prepared. Instead of being blindsided by challenges, wouldn't you rather plan for possible obstacles and then prepare accordingly?

Before a cabin and flight crew is ready to fly, they go through a series of extensive training and practices. Training includes aircraft familiarization, emergency equipment, aircraft systems, and door and window operations. In their training, the importance of communication and teamwork is covered. When experiencing a little, or great, turbulence, how does your team perform? It is not just you, but your organization as a whole, that must be trained to push through. How is your flight plan?

One time, I was not prepared to fly and it almost cost me my life. I encountered unforeseen thunderstorms. Because I was not prepared, I shifted in to instant panic mode. I had previously set the plane on autopilot. It began descending. In my panic, I pulled back on the yoke, but the plane continued to descend, because it was still on autopilot. I wasn't paying attention. I wasn't prepared and as a result, I reacted, instead of appropriately responding. When you are prepared, you respond well, which allows you to relax and keep your mind clear. Reacting can create a greater crisis, in which you don't think straight. Sometimes, you are not rational. My situation was a near-death experience, and I am forever grateful to God for that unforgettable lesson. I could have died, but that just was not my time to go. Life will throw some turbulence in your path, but don't allow reacting to cause your downfall. As a leader, you must remain in the moment and be responsive. The team takes your lead. If you react, then so does your team. But if you respond appropriately, you have a team that remains in control and effective.

I learned something else about reaction versus response. It makes you do some necessary soul searching. When you are distracted, you are not moving forward; in fact, you are actually losing ground. Distractions include busy things on the to-do list or negative thoughts. Anything leading you away and not toward your unlimited possibilities is a distraction. If you want to be successful, learn how to handle and respond to distractions and disruptions.

Death is one of people's top fears. Going through a divorce and bankruptcy follow close behind. Divorce was my disruption or distraction. It was one of the lowest points in my life. A divorce is like a death, in that something that once had life is no more. I blamed myself and started to give up on living. I was merely existing. I turned to alcohol to ease the pain, but it seemed to only put me in a deeper state of despair. I even contemplated suicide. Feeling ashamed, I did not let my family know how low I was. Once I turned back to my faith, God reminded me of the meaning of life. I realized I had been reacting to this disruption and not responding, which in turn had caused me to descend. And the surprising thing was that I didn't even realize how far I had fallen. But in God, I found the meaning of life.

You cannot allow a single event to break your spirit and make you forget the meaning of life. One instance cannot impact your future. With faith, a support system, and the right attitude, you can make it through. Whatever difficulty you may be dealing with does have an end. You can overcome, and your problem does have an expiration date. It is the part of your journey and destiny that is making you stronger.

Though you are ready to take off and be free to travel into your ambitions and aspirations, you have a little more preparation to do. I know you may wonder what else possibly needs to be accomplished. But, I would be careless as your business coach to send you out without a few more tools and ideas to think about that will help guarantee your flourishing life that is to come.

Get Feedback

I've talked already about the danger in having *yes-men* around you. Be cautious of who is in your inner circle of success. To be a great leader, you need to create an environment in which your team members feel empowered to give you their honest input and feedback. If you are viewing things through rose-colored glasses, believing that you are the only one whose opinion matters and that everything you do is perfect, then you will crash and burn. Check your ego at the door and be open to your team's feedback and solutions. "We all need people who will give us feedback. That's how we improve," expressed Microsoft giant Bill Gates. Some have the misconception that leaders have no need to improve. That could not be further from the truth. Team members, including you as the leader, must always be improving. As the leader, you need more improvement than anyone else, as you are the head and decision maker. You improve not only by lessons learned through mistakes and overcoming faults, but also by your organization's feedback.

Feedback analysis provides great insight and helps you manage in the present and in future advancements. Have your team document what their expected outcome(s) from their work will be, say, after a few months or a year. Then, compare that with actual results and achievements. This feedback analysis can be either short or long-term. If things are great, you can still improve upon them. Whatever does not work, implement a proper strategy for the solution.

At times, we are subjective, especially in our own enterprises. But, the views of other members will allow you to make more educated decisions regarding your company.

Your Attitude Determines Your Altitude

Years ago, author, salesman, and motivational speaker Zig Ziglar declared, "It is your attitude, more than your aptitude that will determine your altitude." I could leave it there, as it is self-explanatory, but as a pilot, I have to relate your attitude to your ability to peak. Your attitude is the airplane cockpit. What you say, speak, and think is what controls your transition from the present to your destiny.

When flying and you encounter turbulence, fear kicks in. But, when the pilot's calm voice resounds through the intercom, you feel some assurance that the bumpiness will cease and a smoother ride will ensue. You are the pilot when dealing with obstacles in your life. Talk yourself out of whatever fear you may be experiencing, reestablishing your focal point of what is to be. Though the present situation may be difficult, your future is bright. I am a firm believer that your perspective in life's situations is dictated by attitude—good or bad.

You have probably known or heard of someone receiving a dire prognosis from the doctor that he has only six months to live. If the person's attitude is negative, he might pass sooner. But, if he has a positive attitude and lives life to the fullest, it's possible he could far outlive the six-month estimate. Your attitude regarding your business, time, health, or any situation can determine the outcome. Keep your spirits up and remember to stay responsive and not reactive.

Let Things Go

Don't hold on to past mistakes, disappoints, and failures. You have to release anything that holds you back. You are not your hardships or challenges. Even with properly planning in your purpose, things will come up that will not go exactly as you designed. Let that go. Let it go that you are not in total control and that you have to rely on faith when you encounter the unforeseen. Life is a beautiful thing, but sometimes curveballs come at us to teach invaluable lessons that ultimately contribute to our emotional, mental, and spiritual growth. Just go with the flow of life. Now, I am not saying to go through life expecting bad things to happen, but don't overthink everything, and remember that certain things will be out of your hands a few times in your life. When you do that, you will see that every event can turn out better than you planned.

Prepare for Takeoff

Now you are ready to take off. You should be overjoyed and elated. All of the work you have done thus far has prepared you for this moment. This feeling please hold on to it, and understand that whatever turbulence you may experience on your journey is only temporary. With your positive and productive attitude determining your altitude, there is nothing you cannot handle and no challenge you are not able to be victorious through.

You are in absolute control of when to take off, where you want to take off from, and how far you want to go. You were meant to soar. While in takeoff mode, allow no distractions or disruptions in your universe to move you off of your course. You are flying into your destiny where great things are ahead. I believe it for you, just as you believe it for yourself. You are not on this journey alone, and I am with you every step of the way.

QUESTIONS

1. What disruptions or distractions have been holding you back from taking off to your destiny?

2. How can you overcome them?

3. Have you ever descended? What could you have done differently, and what did you learn in that experience?

4. What is your flight plan for your prosperous life?

5. How has this flight plan allowed you to see and overcome unforeseen challenges?

About the Author

Dr. Charles Kinuthia is a world-renowned wealth and business coach, entrepreneur, speaker, educator, and leader. The same drive and purpose that took him from poverty in Kenya to prosperity is what drives him to help countless people all over the world turn their goals into reality.

With businesses and clients in over seven countries, Charles has taken multiple small businesses to national and international levels of achievement. Exceeding goals and expectations is nothing new to Charles. Recently recognized as one of the fastest growing franchisors in the U.S., he founded **OST Holdings Inc.** in 2009, a tax, accounting, and software firm with locations nationwide, where he serves as the Chief Executive Officer.

Charles is not just a leader in business, but his leadership extends to boards and international organizations. He serves as the Chairperson of the Business Management Advisory Board of **Lone Star College**, the largest community college in Texas. He also serves as an Executive Board Member of **Victorious Living**, a global nonprofit organization dedicated to alleviating poverty through education and the empowerment of small businesses.

From government to business, Charles' training methods transpire across different platforms. For his entrepreneurship and affluence, Charles has been featured on the covers of major publications, including **Franchising USA** and **Entrepreneur** magazines in addition to major news media networks and radio shows all over the world.

Notes

Chapter 1

1. *Dictionary.com*, s.v. "self-reliance," http://www.dictionary.com/browse/self-reliance.

2. *Oxford Dictionary*, s.v. "self-discipline," https://en.oxforddictionaries.com/definition/self-discipline.

Chapter 2

1. *Oxford Dictionary*, s.v. "courage," https://en.oxforddictionaries.com/definition/courage.

Chapter 4

1. *Dictionary.com*, s.v. "imagine," http://www.dictionary.com/browse/imagine?s=t

Chapter 5

1. Tomas Chamorro-Premuzic PhD, "What Makes Your Obsession Healthy or Unhealthy," *Psychology Today*, July 23, 2011, https://www.psychologytoday.com/blog/mr-personality/201107/what-makes-your-obsession-healthy-or-unhealthy.

Chapter 6

1. *Dictionary.com*, s.v. "gift," http://www.dictionary.com/browse/gift?s=t.

Chapter 8

1. Celena Chong, "Blockbuster's CEO once passed up a chance to buy Netflix for only $50 million," July 17, 2015,

http://www.businessinsider.com/blockbuster-ceo-passed-up-chance-to-buy-netflix-for-50-million-2015-7.

www.ingramcontent.com/pod-product-compliance
Lightning Source LLC
Chambersburg PA
CBHW070545090426
42735CB00013B/3073